Child Trauma and Attachment in Common Sense and Doodles

of related interest

**A Therapeutic Treasure Box for Working with Children
and Adolescents with Developmental Trauma**
Creative Techniques and Activities
Dr. Karen Treisman
ISBN 978 1 78592 263 3
eISBN 978 1 78450 553 0

The Simple Guide to Child Trauma
What It Is and How to Help
Betsy de Thierry
Foreword by David Shemmings, Emma Reeves
ISBN 978 1 78592 136 0
eISBN 978 1 78450 401 4

**Attachment-Based Milieus for Healing Child and
Adolescent Developmental Trauma**
A Relational Approach for Use in Settings from Inpatient
Psychiatry to Special Education Classrooms
Jon Stewart
Foreword by Dan Hughes
ISBN 978 1 78592 789 8
eISBN 978 1 78450 739 8

My Life After Trauma Handbook
Bridie Gallagher, Sue Knowles, Reggie Worthington and Jade Baron
Illustrated by Chloe Collett
ISBN 978 1 83997 128 0
eISBN 978 1 83997 129 7

Child Trauma and Attachment in Common Sense and Doodles, Second Edition

A Practical Guide

MIRIAM SILVER

Foreword by Kim S. Golding

Illustrated by Teg Lansdell

Jessica Kingsley Publishers
London and Philadelphia

First edition published in 2013
This edition published in Great Britain in 2023 by Jessica Kingsley Publishers
An imprint of Hodder & Stoughton Ltd
An Hachette Company

1

A CIP catalogue record for this title is available from the British Library and the
Library of Congress

ISBN 978 1 83997 912 5
eISBN 978 1 83997 913 2

Printed and bound in Great Britain by TJ Books Limited

Jessica Kingsley Publishers' policy is to use papers that are natural, renewable
and recyclable products and made from wood grown in sustainable forests. The
logging and manufacturing processes are expected to conform to the environmental
regulations of the country of origin.

Jessica Kingsley Publishers
Carmelite House
50 Victoria Embankment
London EC4Y 0DZ

www.jkp.com

MIX
Paper from
responsible sources
FSC® C013056

Contents

Foreword

As I read Miriam's book, I am especially struck by Chapter 13: Layers. It occurs to me that the book pivots around this chapter. It also makes me smile as the metaphor of layers within a Russian doll are ones that I have used too, but more on that later.

All infants are born authentic. There are no layers. They are tiny bundles of being ready to be taken care of and nurtured. As they mature, the layers begin to develop. How this happens depends on what they are experiencing and how much they need defences because of these experiences. As Miriam explores, for children who have experienced developmental trauma, these layers can be multitude and complex. This allows vulnerability to be hidden whilst the outer layer (painted perfect in Miriam's analogy) is created. In the process the capacity to be and feel authentic is lost.

I have come to understand this even more clearly in my adult therapy work. One of my adult clients, Alexia (not her real name), spent most of her childhood in foster care. She is one of the 'success stories' achieving academic and relational success. And yet when we reflected on our therapy together when she was in her mid-twenties, she told me: 'One of my fears when I started therapy was that I did not know if I was real or not' (Golding and Jones, 2021, p.62).[1]

Just stop and imagine that for a moment:

---

1   Golding, K. S. and Jones, A. (2021) *A Tiny Spark of Hope: Healing Childhood Trauma in Adulthood*. London: Jessica Kingsley Publishers.

Who am I?

- Is this real or just what others want to see?
- Is this real or just a way to keep from being hurt again?
- Is this real or just a defence that allows me to find some way of functioning in the world?

It makes me wonder what our children lose as they struggle to survive in a world of trauma, loss and separation.

Just like Miriam, Alexia and I discovered our own 'Russian doll' to understand the layers she had built to defend her most vulnerable self. We explored what we named as the painted doll built around layers of defences that she needed to survive. We went on to write a book together called *A Tiny Spark of Hope*, and in it we describe how we discovered: 'The resilience and resourcefulness of a child who had to adapt to an adverse early environment. We explore[d] how Alexia, as a child, developed layers of defences in order to make this adaptation, and how as an adult she needed to find a way to move beyond these defences to find the person she was always meant to be. This was a search for authenticity' (p.25).

During our three-year therapeutic journey many questions were raised for me:

- Are we getting it right for children who have experienced developmental trauma – especially those managing the additional trauma of separation and loss of birth family?
- Do children need to grow up feeling inauthentic and unreal, irrespective of how successful they are?
- Whilst children might need the maturity of adulthood to fully process and heal from their early experience, can we find ways to help them with more of this whilst they are growing up?
- Can we do more to understand, parent and support these children in a way that allows them to discover and realise the person they were born to be?

These are questions that Miriam is addressing in this book.

With her clear explanations, supported by many doodles, stories, self-reflections and anecdotes, she helps us to understand the experience of children who have experienced trauma, the impact on brain development, how it is revealed in attachment relationships and the way this is revealed in their behaviours.

She provides ideas for parenting and supporting them differently. She gives us hope that children don't need to grow into adults who need to seek 'therapy because of a need to discover [themselves], to find authenticity', as Alexia did (p.48).

We hold our children's futures in our hands. We share a responsibility to give them the future they deserve, futures where they can be their authentic best. This begins with finding ways to parent and support them for health and well-being. This moves a focus away from behaviour to the whole child.

Child Trauma and Attachment in Common Sense and Doodles provides us with more than a few pointers as to how we can do this.

Kim S. Golding CBE
Clinical psychologist, author and DDP trainer
Worcestershire, England

Acknowledgements

Thanks must first go to my own attachment figures: my wonderful husband, my parents, my children (who have made me do this stuff myself); and to the colleagues I work with at LifePsychol and BERRI.

The material in this book was devised whilst I was running groups for adoptive and foster carers in Northamptonshire. Their feedback, along with comments from colleagues and professionals I have trained, helped the content to evolve and encouraged me to write this book, as I was often asked whether I could provide some more detailed information that people could take away to read in more depth or share with others who were unable to attend the group.

I have also been inspired by attending training, including doing Level One and Level Two of Dan Hughes' training in Dyadic Developmental Psychotherapy and workshops with Kim Golding and with Todd and Melissa Nichols of the Family Attachment Narrative Centre. Finally, I have been involved in running the British Psychological Society network for Clinical Psychologists working with Looked After and Adopted Children (CPLAAC) and more recently as the spokesperson on this topic for the Association of Clinical Psychologists – roles in which I have met many of my peers who are delivering clinical services for and working with populations of children who are looked after and adopted across the United Kingdom. This has been a great chance to share good practice, keep abreast of the latest research and network with those who have written books that have inspired me in my practice.

Preface

This book is intended for foster carers and adoptive parents, kinship carers, teachers, social workers and anyone else who is involved in looking after children who have been placed away from their birth parents to grow up after having experienced early trauma, neglect or abuse.

My aim is to explain in common-sense terms what might be going on for those children and some things that might be useful to do when helping them to make the most of the new parenting they are experiencing and to move on with their lives.

There are many brilliant books out there that give much more technical and detailed explanations of attachment theory, the impact of trauma and different forms of therapeutic models that address these issues (and there is an Additional Reading section at the end so that you can read some of them if you want), but they are often overly complex and not suitable for the lay reader. This book, however, is designed to explain in simple and practical terms the key concepts and how to apply them in real life. I've tried to write in a way that should not be difficult to read and which does not require any previous reading about psychology, attachment or trauma or any specialist knowledge to make sense. I've shared some examples from my own life and people I have worked with[1] to illustrate each

---

[1] The case examples I have used are composite cases. That means that they are anonymised examples made up from several people I have worked with so that they reflect a typical case, rather than one particular individual.

idea and apply it to real life. Most of all, the book should be relevant to the children that you are looking after.

It might help you to know a little bit about my background to help you understand my qualifications and how I came to write the book. I am a consultant clinical psychologist and for the past 25 years I have specialised in working with children and families who have experienced adversity. I've taken a particular interest in working with children who live outside their family of origin, such as children who are in foster care, in adoptive families or living with extended family members, and young people who live in residential placements. I've read a lot of books and scientific papers about attachment, therapy and the impact of trauma and abuse. I've also developed tools to help identify and support the needs of this population[2] and I've conducted my own research in this area, presenting and publishing this as much as I can (although there is still much I'd like to write about).

I've been one of a small but growing group of professionals who have developed specialist expertise in working with attachment relationships and looked after and adopted children, leading an NHS team. I've been an expert witness to the family court in more than 250 cases, where I've assessed children's development and parenting capacity if there has been trauma, maltreatment or concerns about relationships within the family. I've also worked with residential placement providers, supporting their care of some children and young people with complex and challenging needs. Finally, I've done a lot of policy work in this area, contributing to best practice guidance for the National Institute for Health and Care Excellence (NICE) and the Social Care Institute for Excellence (SCIE) and giving evidence to a government select committee, the Independent Care Review and various politicians and policy makers.

My career has given me quite a rounded viewpoint of the experiences that lead young people to become looked after and adopted (e.g., the abuse, neglect and chaotic care that many of them have been through in their lives before the orders were passed and they

---

2   See http://berri.org.uk

were moved to different homes) as well as an understanding of the court process and the outcomes for them in their new homes. While working therapeutically to support children who are in Care or adopted, I have also encountered the kind of difficulties that come up for foster and adoptive carers and have had the privilege of working alongside some of those people to help them form the best possible relationships with their children.

I started out mainly doing consultations for individual families, where I would meet the professionals and the foster/adoptive parents and we would talk about the challenges they faced. It struck me that even though their stories were unique, and their children at different ages and presenting different challenges, many people were experiencing similar types of issues. I ended up often using the same diagrams or 'doodles' that are within this book to explain ideas to many different families. Because of that, I designed, developed and ran a group called Managing Behaviour with Attachment in Mind to teach foster and adoptive parents some of the issues that recurrently came up in consultation.

While many books have been written about attachment, it's my intention for this book to provide a fresh approach by presenting the information in an accessible form. To achieve this, I have made an effort to avoid technical terminology and to be practical, accessible and concise, with numerous doodles to translate information into visual form.

While trying to keep things simple, I've also included signposts for readers who are interested in finding out more. Within the text, there are some numbered references to related academic papers. Brief details of these are listed at the bottom of the page to enable you to find them in the reference list at the end of the book. An Appendix summarises the impact of early trauma, abuse and neglect. I've also included an Additional Reading section, along with a Glossary, although I have also provided explanations within the text when terms are first introduced.

I first wrote this book ten years ago, and I have been delighted that so many people have found it useful. I wanted to update the book to reflect my growing understanding of some areas, which I now see as significant omissions in the original, like the way that grooming and sexual abuse can mislead the fight-or-flight system, and how intersectional adversities can interact to make some populations more vulnerable. It has also given me the opportunity to expand and clarify other areas.

I hope this book of words and doodles offers you plenty to look at and think about, and that you'll give some of the activities a try.

CHAPTER 1

What is Attachment and Why Does it Matter?

Attachment is the nature of a relationship with someone who you love or rely on or whose opinions are important to you. Usually, the primary attachment is between a baby and their parent(s), and it begins before that baby is even born and continues throughout their life. However, you do not usually just have one attachment relationship; you probably have many (this might include your parents, your carers, your grandparents, your teachers, your neighbours, your friends, your partners, your children or other family members), but the first relationships you have often set the template for how other relationships develop.[1]

If your primary carer forms a 'secure base', then the child learns to use that person as a base from which to explore the world. A 'secure base' when it comes to parenting a baby is someone who cares about them and is physically there and interested in the messages that the baby is giving them. They are fairly calm and predictable, do not harm the baby and are not so preoccupied with their own problems (e.g., depression, domestic violence, drug use, alcohol, mental health problems, relationships, work, social media) that they aren't reliably available to interact with the baby. A secure base gives the baby the best chance to learn about themselves, other people and the world in a positive way. It is associated with

---

1 Attachment has categories and impacts on other relationships. See Ainsworth *et al.* (1978).

numerous positive outcomes for the infant, which last throughout that child's life, and makes them more likely to be able to replicate a similar positive experience for their own children if they later become a parent themselves.

As you can see from Doodle 1, a secure base allows the child to learn about the world in a cycle that repeats many times every day. The child leaves the secure base and goes to explore, the exploring makes them anxious and so they seek reassurance by returning to their secure base. One example of that might be when children first come to see me in my clinic (which is similar to behaviour you might have noticed when you have taken a child anywhere new). They might come in holding their parent's hand or clinging on to their leg, and the new environment might be a bit scary – particularly meeting lots of new people – so they might hide behind the parent until they feel a bit more settled and the parent's body language has given them signals that it is safe to go and have a look at the toys in my room. As they begin to settle, they might gradually go and look at the toys but will keep a close watch on the signals their parent is giving. Then I might start talking about the difficulties that have been happening in a family and the child might become a bit more anxious and hide behind their parent for a while, seeking reassurance by returning to their safe base. This cycle might repeat several times during an appointment, but it might repeat a hundred times or more during a day in which a parent is interacting with a baby or a young child.

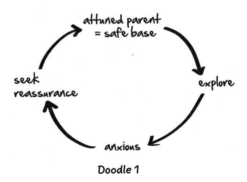

Doodle 1

Even as an adult I continue to use my secure bases. So, for example, if I were to have a sudden rash or illness, I might want to find out about it, so I might look it up on Google or I might book a doctor's appointment. That might make me anxious and therefore I would want to speak to someone who makes me feel secure, like my husband or my parents, in order to feel better before I could then go out and deal with those stresses head on. If you walk home in the dark, particularly if you are a woman, you might want to tell someone you are leaving and when to expect you to be home (or you might talk to someone on a mobile phone as you walk). The person at the other end of that call is acting as your secure base.

When that person who is a secure base is available to the child, predictable and safe, then that cycle leads the child to form what we call a secure attachment pattern. That pattern helps them to form healthy, mutually respectful relationships with others throughout their life and build a good self-image, social skills and empathy. The carer helps to recognise and contain the child's feelings, and to show the child they are loved and worthy of care. Secure infants learn to recognise and regulate their emotions and to recognise which behaviours please their carers and are socially rewarded. Research has shown that secure attachment goes on to be a significant protective factor against a wide range of difficulties. For example, we know that people with secure attachments generally go on to do better at school, in the workplace, in their relationships, in parenting and in their physical health (see the Appendix).

However, not every child is lucky enough to have a parent who can offer a secure base. Some parents are physically or emotionally unavailable for one reason or another. Perhaps they are so depressed that they spend a lot of time zoned out, or they have serious learning disabilities that mean it is harder for them to be sensitive to the needs of the child. Maybe there are major physical or sensory disabilities, or maybe they are using drugs or alcohol. It may be that they are physically not there (interacting with the child) very much because they are working long hours and the quality of childcare is very poor, or they are constantly multitasking, with addictive levels of gambling, internet use, computer games, emails/texts, etc., or they are preoccupied with other stresses in their lives (such as family conflict, domestic violence, harassment, debt, etc.). It may be that they have formed a view that a child is too demanding and have disengaged from them, or they think that putting a child in their room or sitting them in front of the television all day is sufficient parenting. Or maybe the child has to spend a lot of time in hospital or undergoing medical treatment that means they are not able to interact or engage in activities very much. But for whatever reason, even though the primary caregiver does nothing actively harmful to the child (at least not to the extent of physical or sexual abuse, or being severely and repeatedly cruel, critical or rejecting), they are not able to notice and sensitively respond to the signals that their child is giving to them frequently enough to offer that secure base.[2]

If that is the case, then, as you can see from Doodle 2, the child learns one of two patterns to cope with that situation. They either learn to explore and explore and keep on exploring, denying that there is any anxiety (because no reassurance is available) until they become overly self-sufficient and seem fearless and autonomous beyond their years. Or they do the opposite and constantly seek reassurance but never feel reassured (because the reassurance is not effective) and so become very clingy and dependent.

Children in that fearless and overly self-sufficient group can often seem mature and independent beyond their years. They can be quiet and undemanding or may be quite rejecting of nurture and unwilling to show any feelings or vulnerability. They might deny all anxiety and seem fearless about things that are dangerous in the world. They may either present as needing very little adult care or end up so fearless and tough that they are considered 'beyond parental control'. In attachment terminology those children are known as 'insecure avoidant' – they avoid attachment relationships because they are not accustomed to being able to use the secure base for reassurance.

---

2 Some parents are not attuned to a baby's signals (e.g., due to mental health problems, learning disabilities or preoccupation with other things). See Cleaver, Unell and Aldgate (1999) and Reder and Lucey (2000).

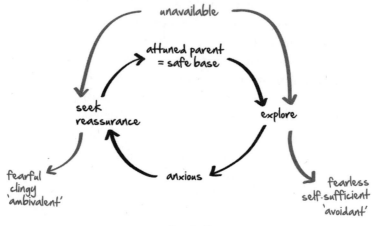

Doodle 2

On the other hand, when the child goes the other way and becomes very clingy, they will often present as immature and needy. They constantly seek the reassurance and nurture they require but because the parent is unable to provide this secure base, they do not feel reassured enough to be able to engage in the normal process of exploring and gradually gaining independence. The parent is perhaps too anxious, depressed or intrusive to allow the child sufficient autonomy to explore, so the child learns to be dependent, immature and needy. In attachment terminology these children are referred to as 'insecure ambivalent' because they want their attachment relationships to reassure them but they do not feel reassured.

Both being 'avoidant' and being 'ambivalent' are sensible, consistent patterns for dealing with the type of attachment figure that a child has experienced and they are quite widespread in the general population. These two patterns are called 'insecure but organised' attachments. They are not as protective as having a secure attachment relationship, but they are not as damaging as the final category of attachment relationship ('insecure disorganised', described in the next paragraph), because the parent is at least fairly consistent and not actively harmful, so the child can at least learn ways of dealing with the world that gain a predictable response. Therefore, although these relationships are not following the ideal template, they should not automatically be seen as harmful or pathological, as they are relatively prevalent and not outside the range of normal relationships. However, within each category there is a range of presentations, and the less there has been a secure attachment figure available and the greater the other needs of the child (e.g., if they also have a learning disability or a neurodevelopmental disorder), the more likely that child is to need additional support in order to thrive.

The final category involves parents who provide care that is chaotic, unpredictable or at times harmful towards the child. This would include any parents who are physically abusive, sexually abusive, emotionally abusive or chronically neglectful to an extent that endangers the child. It would also include parents who are so busy surviving their own chaotic lives, filled with substance abuse and/or domestic violence and/or conflict and stress, that the child's needs take low priority and the child is exposed to the chaotic, conflict-ridden environment that surrounds them. That may mean they are exposed to other dangers, such as bullying, grooming, abuse, exploitation, or involved in crime, violence or substance misuse.

Children in this category are known as 'insecure disorganised' because no single 'organised' strategy would help them to feel safe the way it does in the organised insecure patterns. As you can see from Doodle 3, they therefore learn to make the best of each situation, treating each adult differently to get their needs met. This might lead children like this to be described as manipulative, fake, provocative or attention seeking. They might also have learnt to be superficially charming (particularly to those other than their main attachment figure). They also have a tendency to reach rage (an out-of-proportion level of anger) more quickly, without an obvious reason or in response to seemingly minor provocation. I'll talk more about this when we come to discuss 'fight or flight' in Chapter 5.

Each of these strategies makes sense in the context of the children's lives. So if, for example, a stranger is more likely to give a child food, attention or comfort than their parent, they would learn to approach strangers in ways that are likely to get their needs met, by being charming or by being babyish, by pulling on their sympathy, or by trying to meet the needs of the adult in some way that they would reward. Similarly, if it is hard to get any attention in your environment, you learn to do the things that cannot be ignored, the things that really press people's buttons. Phrases like 'attention seeking' really mean that the child is having to work hard to get their needs met, and has learnt to express them indirectly or in less socially acceptable ways. Labels like 'manipulative' mean that the child tries different strategies with different people to try to get their needs met. All of these strategies are adaptive responses to abnormal experiences and make the child extremely vulnerable.[3]

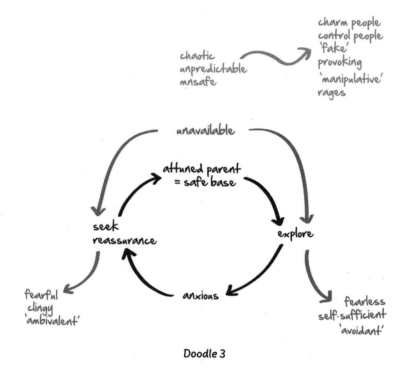

Doodle 3

Children who have experienced abuse react in different ways. They may internalise their distress and become withdrawn, anxious or depressed. Or they may act out their feelings in challenging

---

3   Disorganised attachment is a normal response to abuse and has poor outcomes. See Carlson *et al.* (1989), van IJzendoorn, Schuengel and Bakermans Kranenburg (1999) and Zeanah, Keyes and Settles (2003).

behaviour or risk-taking. Sexual abuse may lead to sexualised behaviours. Neglect may show in developmental delays. These external signs of dysfunction are often closely connected to mental health, self-esteem and patterns of interpersonal relationships.

Sadly, these behaviour patterns are also more common in children who live in war zones, are homeless or part of marginalised communities, or in children who undergo dangerous journeys to migrate to countries where their families believe they will be safer or have better life chances – because there is very real threat and the focus is on day-by-day survival, meaning that the adults do not always have the emotional capacity to offer a secure attachment. Children who require repeated painful medical treatments early in their lives are also at greater risk of attachment difficulties and post-traumatic stress (even with loving parents). These are all part of the spectrum of 'chronic developmental trauma' – the process of growing up in an environment with recurrent threat or harm. Whilst there may be many overlaps in the core themes of threat and trauma, and I hope that there will be things in this book that are helpful if you are supporting or caring for a child who has been through these experiences, each of these scenarios has specific unique elements that may shape the impact on the child that will not be covered in any depth as my focus in this book is primarily on children who are exposed to harm within their family or social network.

🔆 Reflection: Spotting your own patterns now

Have a look at the cycle diagrams in Doodles 1–3 and see which one you identify with as reflecting your own relationships with different people. Is there someone you use as a secure base and go to when you feel stressed? Are there times when you feel pushed towards being more avoidant or more ambivalent?

Normally when we're under stress we all have times in which we react in one way or the other. For me, the most obvious example I can think of is when my husband was made redundant and we moved to a new area. I really did not want to make him feel guilty about us needing to relocate so I wanted to show him that everything was fine. I didn't want to approach him with my stresses because it would have felt like I was unfairly burdening him at a difficult time or blaming him for my feelings. So I would smile and act like everything was fine. I'd smile and say, 'Oh we're moving away from the area where I know lots of people to an area where I know no one? That's fine, it will be for the best. I'm moving from a job where I know everybody, I know my routines and I'm enjoying everything that I do to a place where everything will be new? That's fine, don't worry. We're moving from the house I built my nest in to a house that needs doing up and has no kitchen, bathroom or central heating yet? That's fine, don't worry, it'll be a fun project.' So I started a new job, in a new town, in a new house, without the support of my friends and family around, and denied the emotional impact of that. I put on a good show and didn't burden anyone with guilt or moaning. I wore a smiley face and carried on being a competent psychologist and a supportive wife, and I kept all those negative feelings to myself. That's an example of an avoidant attachment style under stress.

I realised after about a year that only showing one facet of my feelings to the people around me meant that all my relationships felt insincere and lacking in depth, and I began to be more honest with people. I told my husband that whilst I didn't blame him for moving, it had been a very hard process for me to adjust to and that I had been feeling quite sad and isolated. He responded in a very sincere and empathic way. It was reassuring to know that the people I care about didn't crumble under the additional stress I placed upon them, and my relationships grew back to being as strong and secure as they had always felt. It was a very helpful learning experience for me because it now helps me to empathise more effectively with those children who have come from one home to another and are trying to present a pleasing but slightly false-feeling persona so that they are liked in the new placement; this is something we will come back to in Chapter 13.

Reflection: Spotting your own childhood patterns
Think about your own childhood relationships and whether there
was anyone around who led you to feel less secure or who treated
you badly. What impact do you think that has had on you? What
made the impact more or less significant for you?

When it comes to attachment relationships, particularly friendships
and romantic partners, we tend to seek out people with a similar or
complementary attachment style to ourselves. Those first formative
relationships are important in setting the template for the relationships that will follow. For example, it is common, in my experience,
for anxious dependent people to pair up with someone strong but
avoidant. If you have a secure base during childhood, then you are
able to seek out people who will form positive, respectful, mutually
beneficial relationships. But we all come across people who are chaotic and harmful and carry a disorganised attachment pattern, so it
can be that we have a mixture of attachment styles influencing our
lives at different times. Where those relationships are transitory
or happen later in your life you can normally recognise them as
negative relationships and avoid them, keeping your main template
of relationships as the ones that are more secure. We know from
research that any one secure relationship in a person's childhood
is incredibly protective, even when other relationships are insecure
(even insecure disorganised).

Attachment and trauma are closely intertwined, because
trauma increases the risk of disorganised attachment, and lack of
secure attachment relationships makes children more vulnerable
to being victims of abuse and trauma. Having a primary attachment
relationship in the insecure disorganised category is something
that can have a profound effect. Children who are classified as
having insecure disorganised attachment styles do much worse
in all kinds of biological, psychological and social outcomes. They
tend to do worse in school and in employment, they have a higher
risk of substance abuse or involvement in crime, more risk of
relationship breakdown, more difficulties with parenting and risk
of their own children being taken into Care, more risk of mental

health problems and even more risk of physical problems such as cancer, heart disease and diabetes. There are clinicians and researchers who would argue that almost all challenging behaviour seen in the home and the school relates to poor early care and attachment experiences.[4]

There is a huge body of research now about the impact of Adverse Childhood Experiences, known as ACEs. The Adverse Childhood Experiences study (Felitti et al., 1998) was a huge and ground-breaking study that showed that the impact of childhood adversity is cumulative and long-lasting.[5] It showed that the more negative experiences a child has within their family (such as abuse, neglect, domestic violence, parental separation, parental alcohol/ substance misuse, parental mental health problems), the more this makes them vulnerable to a variety of negative social and health outcomes. However, it is important to understand that these risks don't make negative outcomes inevitable, no matter how many ACEs a child has experienced. In fact, the majority of people who have experienced high levels of ACEs still go on to be healthy and have good lives. When we look at why some children come through difficult experiences better than others, some of that is to do with biological factors (genetics, exposure to drugs or alcohol during pregnancy or the presence of physical or intellectual disabilities). However, I believe that the most critical thing that determines whether children with high levels of ACEs go on to experience negative outcomes is whether they have at least one positive relationship, and whether that person can recognise and meet their psychological needs, as this is a powerful protective factor. We will explore that in more depth in the next chapter.

You may be wondering what percentages of the general population fall into the different attachment categories. As you can see from Doodle 4, studies generally say that around 50 per cent

---

4   Trauma underlies most disruptive behaviour. See Dodge, Bates and Pettit (1990), Sansone, Furukhi and Wiederman (2012) and Wolfe *et al.* (2003).

5   The Centers for Disease Control and Prevention (CDC) has a summary of the numerous findings on its website: www.cdc.gov/violenceprevention/aces/index. html

of people are in the secure category, around 40 per cent are in the insecure but organised categories and around 10 per cent are in the insecure disorganised category, though this really varies from study to study depending on the population, the age at which it is measured and the methodology.[6]

	General	In Care
secure	50–60%	> 10% ?
organised but insecure	30–40%	40% ?
disorganised insecure	10%	50% ?

Doodle 4

However, it is worth noticing that children in the Care system are very skewed in this distribution; it seems very unlikely that there are significant numbers of children in the secure category because, by definition, children in the Care system have had separation from their first caregivers and have often been through neglect or abuse and multiple changes of placement. From my experience of working with looked after and adopted children during the past decade and my understanding of the research literature, I would suggest their percentages are probably pretty much a reverse pattern of what you see in the general population. Based on research with children exposed to trauma, under 10 per cent of looked after children are securely attached at the point that they arrive in a new placement, around 40 per cent of children arriving in placement are insecure but organised and around 50 per cent of children (particularly those in residential care or who have had multiple placement changes) would reach that disorganised category.[7] The prevalence of the more dysfunctional attachment patterns is not surprising because, of course, looked after and adopted children make up less than 1 per

---

6 Proportions of children in the attachment categories in the general population. See van IJzendoorn *et al.* (1999).
7 Proportions in different attachment categories amongst traumatised/looked after children. See van IJzendoorn *et al.* (1999).

cent of children and are only taken from the 1 per cent of families in the wider population where there have been the most disruptive and damaging experiences going on around them.

Whilst there is a lot of individual variation – depending on the type and extent of any abuse, whether or not there were any protective relationships, the child's development, personality and preferences, and the personalities, skills and expectations of the caregivers – in my experience, the distribution of attachment styles is closely tied in to the child's route through the Care system. Children who are removed very early, and/or who have experienced mild or short-term exposure to abuse or chaotic environments, tend to have more organised attachments. They typically settle very well and are most likely to end up with very stable long-term relationships through adoption or long-term fostering. Children who have been exposed to more severe and enduring abuse, neglect and chaotic care, including those who have moved in and out of care, or through many different living arrangements and primary carers within their birth family before they are removed, tend to have more disorganised attachments. As a result, adoption is much less likely to be possible, and whilst foster care can be an option for permanence, they may find it harder to settle in a new family and are more likely to experience subsequent moves or placement breakdown.

Those who have experienced the most severe trauma, abuse and neglect over the most prolonged periods of time, and/or the most changes of caregiver (with the accompanying experiences of loss and rejection), are more likely to end up in a residential placement. This might happen after multiple foster placements break down, or they may come into Care in adolescence and end up in a children's home or supported accommodation setting as a suitable foster placement cannot be identified to meet their needs. The sad thing is that the children who have experienced the greatest negative impact from early exposure to trauma and dysfunctional relationships also end up being the most likely to end up with additional moves or living in a situation in which they don't have a full-time primary carer but a rotating staff team. Thus the Care system can further compound attachment issues by providing less stable attachment relationships for the very children who need them most.

There is a lot of unhelpful language used to describe issues around attachment and trauma. Attachments are often described as 'weak' or 'strong', which is very unhelpful, as sometimes the strongest feelings are evoked by unhealthy relationships. Likewise, professionals can evaluate parenting as if any negative elements can be weighed up against the positive elements. However, no matter how nice the positive times are, this can never undo the impact of abuse or neglect, or the way that being exposed to trauma affects the development of the child. The first key question always has to be whether the person is likely to cause the child further harm, and the second is whether they can help the child to recover from the harm they have already experienced. There can be non-abusing parents who have failed to protect a child from an abusive partner, who can separate from that relationship and go on (with support and personal therapy) to be protective parents. But there are also parents who love their children but are unable to keep them safe or to help them recover, perhaps because of their own traumatic experiences or mental health. The professionals always need to act in the child's best interests. I think most people working in children's health and social care want to do that, but sometimes dysfunctional systems can get in the way. Perhaps their perspective is skewed by their own experiences, by the availability or price of certain types of services or placements or by the policies of their agency. So you may have to advocate for your child's needs and try several different people or organisations before finding the help that you need.

There is also the question of diagnosis, as some clinicians will diagnose 'attachment disorder' in a particular child. The two most popular diagnostic classification systems in the world describe two distinct forms of attachment disorder: 'reactive attachment disorder' and 'disinhibited social engagement disorder/disinhibited attachment disorder'. The first involves the inability to attach to a preferred caregiver (which can be thought of as too little attachment-seeking), and the second involves indiscriminate sociability and disinhibited attachment behaviours (which can be thought of as too much attachment-seeking, in the wrong places). I tend to avoid these labels, as I do not believe that any form of attachment difficulty is a disorder that can be identified in the child as an individual in isolation. Attachment disorder is a pattern that plays out between that child and the people around them, particularly their primary caregiver(s). I also think that it is very important that the label does not imply that there is an organic underlying condition the child was born with, as I see attachment disorder as being a normal response to abnormal circumstances and not something innate to the child. As such, I tend to favour Bessel van der Kolk's view of Chronic Developmental Trauma as a subcategory of post-traumatic stress.[8]

---

8   See van der Kolk (2005).

CHAPTER 2

Can Attachment Patterns Change?

It is incredible to think what a profound effect the parenting you receive in the first two years of life can have on such a wide-ranging number of outcomes (a brief summary of the impact of poor early care is given in the Appendix, complete with references to some of the scientific studies). We also know that the longer a child is left in a chaotic home without secure attachment relationships, the more difficult it is to change the patterns later and the more challenging it becomes to help that child get onto a better trajectory for their adult relationships.[1]

However, even children whose primary relationship is insecure disorganised do not inevitably go on to have that attachment pattern for life. In fact, there is a significant group of adults who, when studied, have a fifth attachment classification known as 'earned secure' (or 'learned secure'). These individuals have used other relationships in their lives to recognise and reflect that the pattern they have learnt from their parents is not the only one available and was not the quality of care that they deserved or want to replicate. They have been able to use a secure base in later life to learn how to become one themselves.[2] That learning experience can be from one consistent caregiver during childhood (even if they are a grandparent, uncle, aunt or sibling rather than a primary carer), a foster

---

1   The longer a child is left in chaos/trauma, the harder it is to recover. See Felitti *et al.* (1998) and Glaser (2001).
2   See Saunders *et al.* (2011).

or adoptive parent, a close friendship, an adult relationship or even the therapeutic relationship with a counsellor or psychologist or other professional in the mental health sector that they have seen over an extended period of time. That is why hope is not lost even when someone has had an awful start in life, and it is so valuable when people recognise their own difficulties and seek out the right support in order to think about and change their own attachment pattern to a more organised or secure one. Even the relationship that a child has with a teacher, social worker, neighbour, support worker or someone they interact with regularly through a shared activity (e.g., within a sports club, religious group, or the parent of a friend) can be a template of a healthier relationship and have a positive impact.

The people in the 'earned secure' category can go on to be quite resilient in their parenting and their relationships; nearly as much so as the people who had secure relationships in their childhood to begin with.[3] This represents a powerful message of hope because it means that anybody can change their attachment style and there is never a point at which it is too late to change, though obviously the earlier the better. There are increasing numbers of therapists who are able to recognise and work with children and adults whose early care and attachment experiences have been poor, in order to help them develop these 'earned secure' qualities and challenge their patterns of thinking and behaviour. This can enable them to form healthier relationships and a more positive sense of themselves, others and the world.

☼ Reflection: Positive ripples

Who do you see as the most positive role models in your life? Would you want to parent like either or both of your parents or somebody different? Are there other people who have been impor-tant in your life? Did you have a favourite teacher or adult leader? Or a best friend that really stuck by you? How about things people

---

3   Earned secure outcomes are nearly equivalent to secure. See Lichtenstein Phelps, Belsky and Crnic (1998).

have said that have stayed with you? Have you ever been regarded as a role model by someone else? Or thanked by someone else for making a difference in their life? How did that feel?

I had a remarkable experience recently when somebody contacted me through social media. She told me that she had come to see me as a child, 20 years ago, and had a very positive memory of the experience. She said that at the time she felt worthless but, 'You saw me as a person and spoke to me like I was worth something. I could feel that and it mattered a great deal to me.' She has gone on to train as a mental health professional, and told me she aims to pass that feeling on to other young people. Her message really made my day. It is a helpful reminder that any moment of human connection and empathy can create positive ripples that continue to spread out into the world. And if you have taken the time to read a book about how to support children who have experienced trauma, abuse and neglect, I am confident that you will be creating similar ripples in the people that you love and care for.

One of the things that predicts whether you will be an optimal parent who can ensure your child is secure is your ability to recognise the links between childhood experiences and the kind of person that child becomes later in their life.[4] Generally, people who say 'I was smacked all the time and it didn't do me any harm' haven't really reflected on their own experiences as much as would be necessary to draw that conclusion.

In my therapeutic work I've met children and adults with a multitude of different responses to the trauma and neglect they have experienced in their life. Some adults are incredibly worried about their ability to parent and how to do the job of parenting differently to the parenting that they experienced in their own childhood. I view that anxiety as a good sign! Being concerned about how to parent as well as your child deserves is really natural and something that most people experience at some point. This is true even for people who have had great upbringings and who have given birth to children

---

4   See Fonagy, Steele and Steele (1991) and Slade (2005).

who don't have any difficulties. If you have experienced adversity, then it's a really positive sign to be actively thinking about how to do something different and how to not keep following the patterns that are familiar. It is this active reflection that leads people to becoming more secure and able to provide better care and more emotional attunement to their children than they experienced themselves. However, it's hard work to consciously parent your children differently to how you grew up, compared with simply following the familiar patterns formed by the way you were parented!

The parents who cause me concern are the ones who clearly had very poor care in their own childhood but have later come to accept, normalise or even idealise this. They describe their childhoods as being happy and their parents as being caring and loving, even when the evidence shows they were abused and neglected. It is this (perhaps unconscious) desire to squash the negative memories of the past, downgrade the importance of their unhappy feelings and whitewash over problems that suggests these parents do not recognise the shortcomings in their own experience and are thus not able to reflect on how they need to improve things and can end up repeating familiar patterns.

Case example: A worthless man

I recently spoke to a man whose partner wanted them to try for a baby. He felt that he would 'never be ready to be a father'. He reported feeling 'depressed, useless and a failure' all of his adult life. He said that other people perceived him as either distant or angry but that he was simply responding to perceived criticism, as he thought they looked down on him. He told me that he desperately wanted to be loved but that his girlfriend and prior partners found him 'too emotional but in all the wrong ways'. He thought this had nothing to do with his childhood, which he said was 'fine' and 'as good as anyone else's' and 'not an excuse for my failure'.

As we formed a greater level of trust, I learned that his parents had very traditional gender roles and were domestically violent throughout his childhood. He was frequently criticised as a young boy, particularly when he expressed any needs or showed any distress, and was told that 'boys don't cry' and to 'be a man', which he took to mean to be more like his (violent and controlling) father. He had learned that responding with anger to parental criticism made him feel stronger and less vulnerable and to shut off emotionally and detach himself from others. Although he still felt worthless inside, he had learned to hide this behind a façade of not caring or, when pressed, his anger, which had caused him to lose relationships and jobs in the past. He was sceptical that anyone could find anything loveable about him and struggled to really trust anyone else with his feelings. The idea of having a baby was terrifying to him, as a baby would have needs he would be expected to fulfil, and he did not feel able to provide the necessary care. We worked on using our therapeutic relationship as a model of trust and being valued to help build his self-image.

Case example: A soft mother

I recently worked with a mother who was having difficulties providing any boundaries and structure for her child. She found it really difficult to set any rules or demonstrate any consequences if her child failed to follow her instructions. Because of this, her child's behaviour was quite disruptive and oppositional, and the school had to involve their behaviour and inclusion team in an effort to stop the child from being excluded from mainstream lessons.

When we explored the mother's history, it emerged that she had been physically abused by her stepfather and her mother had been very 'soft' with her to compensate for this but had never intervened to protect the children. The woman had learnt that there were only two ways to parent – being punitive and abusive or being soft and ineffective, and she did not want to be the former. We worked together to see that there was plenty of scope to be an assertive and caring parent without adopting either of these two extremes and that the best parents are able to provide some boundaries and consequences to help to shape a child's behaviour and prepare them for functioning well in the world. Setting limits for her children did not make her similar to her father.

Being a parent is a huge responsibility because you are shaping the life of a person. Many people find that when they have a child and feel how overwhelming that responsibility is, their views about parenting change a lot. They feel huge amounts of guilt when they think that they haven't got it right for the vulnerable little person who is totally dependent on them and who they love more than they ever thought possible. However, the standards that most caring parents believe they should aspire to are much closer to perfection than is required. Provided that you are able to love a child, see them as an individual, give them positive feedback and offer them developmentally appropriate stimulation, you are likely to be doing a good job.

However, the aim of this book is to help you fine-tune those intuitive (and perhaps well-practised) parenting skills to meet the needs of children who have experienced early trauma and poor care. The demands of 're-parenting' such children are much greater than of parenting a birth child who has not experienced such stressors.[5] Hopefully, the rest of the book will help you think about what is different about children who have experienced abuse, neglect and chaotic or harmful early care, and what you can do to assist such children to recover from those experiences and go on to be healthy, happy young people who form successful relationships with others.

The first challenge, however, is to recognise the attachment patterns that your child brings with them and to gently act in a way that brings them towards your secure pattern (and to seek help and support to reach a secure position, or to return there if you ever feel pulled out of your secure pattern). To do this we need to work out what their underlying need is as well as the expressed

---

5   See Appleyard and Osofsky (2003) and Banyard, Rozelle and Englund (2001).

need. For example, a child who has an ambivalent attachment style will strongly express their need for reassurance, but they may need to be given a message that it is okay to learn to explore. On the other hand, a child who is avoidant will seem self-sufficient and will explore but won't be keen to return to have reassurance and nurture. But this unexpressed need being met is what will help them to become more secure, so it will be beneficial for them if you can find ways to offer reassurance and comfort, even when they don't ask for this overtly.

If the child is insecure disorganised, then it might be that they present different needs to different people or express their needs in very dysfunctional and indirect ways. The most helpful strategy might be to begin to name the needs that are being expressed so that they are acknowledged directly and to offer a level of consistency and understanding they have not experienced before. For example, it might be that you can say 'I think you are feeling a bit worried about this' even if they are showing difficult behaviour rather than anxiety in a new situation. Whatever the child's pattern is, it is really useful to have a think about both the expressed and unexpressed needs so that you are not unintentionally reinforcing unhelpful patterns. Kim Golding writes brilliantly about this.[6]

MEASURING EARLY ATTACHMENT

Researchers can reliably pick up which attachment category children fall into by 12 months of age by putting them through the Strange Situation task.[7] The researchers observe how the infant responds to separation from their parent and what they do when they are reunited. What is amazing about attachment is that it isn't a quality of an individual in isolation. The components of that infant's personality, or any organic conditions they might have, affect their attachment pattern remarkably little. We know this because attachment does not magically appear when the child appears, complete

---

6   See Golding (2008).
7   See Ainsworth *et al.* (1978).

with their personal characteristics.[8] Researchers can do the Adult Attachment Interview with expectant mothers during pregnancy, and by talking to them and hearing about their ways of understanding the world, they can already predict which kind of attachment style the child is going to have in two thirds of cases. This is really important because it tells us something about the fact that attachment is not innate in a child; it is a response to their experiences and their relationships. This also gives us clues about attachment patterns being transmitted from generation to generation.

One of the things that we know from studying the attachment classifications of parents and the subsequent attachment patterns of their children is that parents who have experienced poor care themselves are much more likely to go on and recreate a similar attachment style (or an equally dysfunctional attachment style) with their children.[9] What is interesting, however, is that attachment style is not completely fixed and continues to respond to the experiences and relationships you have throughout life.[10] So if someone 'inherits' a reasonable attachment template from a parent whose attachment style was organised insecure (which is quite common and not pathological), that person might get into a relationship that then somehow goes downhill (e.g., because there is some drug use or domestic violence or the partner's mental health deteriorates). That might gradually undermine their self-image more and more until they are functioning in a very chaotic way. If they have a baby at this point, their child may then be insecure disorganised and therefore do worse in attachment terms than the parent's attachment experience would suggest.

Equally, however, it may be that parents who have come out of very destructive patterns, and as children had very insecure or disorganised attachment patterns, can come away and reflect on that later and form more stable relationships into which they

---

8   See Fonagy *et al.* (1991) and van IJzendoorn (1995).
9   Parents' attachment styles influence the infant's attachment style. See van IJzendoorn, Juffer and Duyvesteyn (1995).
10   See Caltabiano and Thorpe (2007).

have a child. Or they might have one protective relationship with a teacher, neighbour or grandparent who models for them a more secure pattern that they can then draw on as a parent. Or they might as an adult go and seek therapy and the therapist might provide that secure relationship or a sounding board against which to test out the thoughts, feelings, behaviours and beliefs that they have learnt from early life. In any of these scenarios they may go on, despite this very difficult background, to be able to parent in a much more secure way. As I mentioned above, in attachment research we call those people earned secure (or learned secure).

A lot of research literature shows that people who are in the earned secure group actually do nearly as well at parenting as people whose childhoods gave them a secure classification in the first place. In my view, when you look at secure versus earned secure, people who are in the earned secure category are very resilient, as they are used to challenges and overcoming them but have more buttons to press from their own history. On the other hand, people who are in the secure category may have had a very quiet, easy life and not have been confronted by those challenges. This means they may not have acquired the level of resilience of those in the earned secure group, but out of all the attachment groups they have the strongest innate pattern and the fewest buttons to press that could affect their parenting.

In my experience (supported by several research studies), adoptive and foster parents and care professionals often fall into either the secure or earned secure groups,[11] but which one of these it is gives them different characteristics. People who have experienced secure attachments have a lot of empathy, so they often feel that they have had a lucky life and want to help others who have not been so lucky. On the other hand, people who have had a really tough set of early experiences often feel profoundly grateful to the individuals who have offered them healthy and loving relationships that allowed them to process their experiences, and want to take

---

11 See Caltabiano and Thorpe (2007).

on that role for others. Both groups can be very motivated to help children who have had a challenging start in life, and each brings considerable strengths to the role. That is why I think it is quite interesting really to look at how those patterns work and think about where you fit in. You can probably recognise yourself in bits of these descriptions, and it is good to reflect on what patterns you bring to the relationship, as this increases your resilience. It is also worth remembering that under stress we can all tip one way or the other, even if we are secure. It is well known, for example, that health concerns, employment changes such as redundancy, relationship breakdown and other major life events make people less secure, though this change is normally temporary.[12]

Research highlights certain qualities that are associated with going on to become earned secure;[13] one is being the kind of person who reflects a lot on life. I think sometimes that is an intuitive thing and sometimes that is learnt from the people around you. Being intelligent is quite protective because it lets you reflect and observe that things are different in other families. But having models somewhere in your life repertoire of what secure relationships are like is also very protective, so no matter how chaotic your life is, your outcomes are almost always better if you have one or two good relationships than if you have only had negative disruptive relationships.[14] That is why it is so important that we acknowledge and give credit to the fact that a good relationship with a teacher, neighbour or grandparent, and definitely one with a foster carer or adoptive parent, can actually turn around a child's life. One secure attachment relationship can be amazingly powerful.

---

12 Attachment style changes under stress (e.g., with infertility or if in a domestic violence relationship). See Burns (1990), Hart and McMahon (2006), McMahon *et al.* (1999) and Rothman (1986).

13 Earned secure is related to intelligence, reflective functioning or other qualities of the individual. See Bond and Bond (2004), Fonagy *et al.* (1994) and Saunders *et al.* (2011).

14 See Gass, Jenkins and Dunn (2007) and Werner and Smith (1992).

Reflection: Recognising attachment styles

Try to think about your own attachment relationships and what has influenced your attachment style over time. When have you been more or less secure? Now think about the child you care for. What may have influenced their attachment style? How would you wish to influence it? What barriers might there be in doing this?

CHAPTER 3

What is 'Good Enough' Care, and What Does it Do?

A good carer can provide a safe and reasonably predictable environment in which to bring up their baby. They give enough attention to notice the signals the baby communicates when they are feeling hungry, feeling tired, have wind, are unwell or have done a wee or poo in their nappy and will try to resolve that by providing appropriate food, rest, burping or treatment, keeping them clean and changing their nappy. A good carer will notice the temperature and check that the baby is appropriately dressed or covered. They will provide soothing movements and skin contact by cradling, cuddling, rocking, stroking or patting, along with talking or singing to the baby in order to help calm them if they are distressed or soothe them to sleep if they are tired. They will interact with the baby in a way that is engaging and stimulating but at an appropriate level to the baby's development. The food they provide will also be tailored to the baby's developmental stage and their individual needs. The clothing they provide will fit comfortably and be kept relatively clean. They will wash the baby sufficiently frequently and be observant to any signs of ill health.

Importantly, they will recognise psychological and emotional need as well as providing physical care. They will take pleasure in interacting with the baby and show that they care about them. They will allow the developing infant to explore within a safe and reasonably clean environment and be careful to ensure that other people who interact with the baby will do so safely and in a way that doesn't cause the baby distress. They will give the baby enough time with a limited group of (typically one to four) specific individuals so that the baby can start to recognise them and form relationships. And as the infant starts to develop, a good carer will help them to recognise their own feelings by naming them and to recognise the feelings of others by exaggerating their own facial expressions and vocal tone when expressing feelings towards the infant. They will give the infant increasing autonomy and provide a variety of experiences to encourage their developing social confidence.

We can think of all of these experiences as bricks in the wall of experiences required for healthy development (see Doodle 5). Amazingly, these simple and frequently intuitive ways to care for a baby are all that it takes to help the baby's brain develop and for their map of the world to be formed on the basis that they are a loveable individual, that other people are generally good and that the world is an interesting and mainly safe place to live.[1] This is the basis of a secure attachment and optimal development.

Case example: Nursery rhymes

I went to observe a contact session (family time) between a nine-year-old boy called Oliver and his grandparents. I arrived first, and then Oliver was brought by his social worker. We were put in a room where the session was to take place to wait for his grandparents' arrival. The room was quite sparsely furnished and had very few toys, none that were age appropriate for Oliver. On the wall were posters of nursery rhymes that also seemed too babyish given his age. I commented that there wasn't much in the room to do and asked if I should go and get some books and toys. Before I got up, Oliver asked me what the poster on the wall was about, pointing to a dark-blue print with yellow text and a starry sky. I said, 'It's Twinkle Twinkle Little Star.' He looked at me blankly. I added, 'You know, the nursery rhyme.' He still looked blank, so I read the beginning of it: 'Twinkle twinkle little star, how I wonder what you are.' He smiled and said, 'Read it!', so I read him the

---

1   Good care leads to adaptive and positive core beliefs. See Wearden *et al.* (2008).

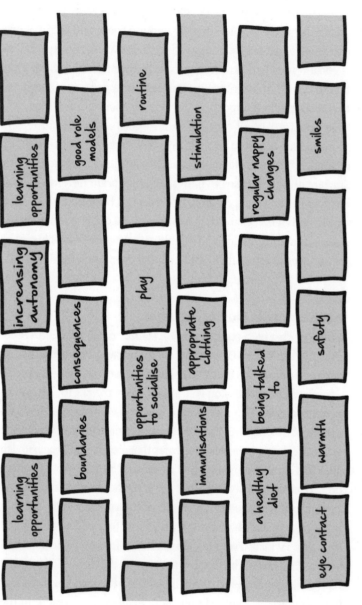

Doodle 5

whole rhyme. Then he pointed at the next picture and said, 'What's that?' I said, 'It's Baa Baa Black Sheep.' He said, 'Read it!', so I did. He then pointed at the next picture, and the next, making me read each of the five nursery rhymes to him twice. I then noticed that we were 20 minutes past the agreed time and his grandparents had not attended. I informed the centre, who contacted Oliver's social worker to collect him. I went back into the room to wait with him, and he asked me to read some of the nursery rhymes again. He was clearly unfamiliar with all of them, and the simple activity of reading to him was something that kept his rapt attention for more than half an hour, despite their simplicity and typically being pitched to a much younger child. I felt like I learnt a lot about Oliver's family from that half an hour. But I also learnt that I can't assume that all children will have experienced things I previously considered to be almost universal in bringing up a child in this country, like reciting nursery rhymes, or reading to a child and tucking them into bed at night. His unfamiliarity with nursery rhymes and delight at sharing a playful activity with an adult showed me how much he was crying out for simple nurture from a caregiver. When I read all the paperwork, it turned out that my impression was consistent with lots of documented evidence of neglect. Oliver had often been left locked in his room, or home alone, and his mother had been preoccupied with her own needs. Sadly, this was not the first time that members of his family had not attended family time or informed anyone that they were not coming (despite there being no emergency to keep them away), but it was clear how ready he was to make up for lost time with a new caregiver.

Parenting is a really important task and a big responsibility. The quality of care that a child receives in early childhood is a powerful determinant of how they will feel about themselves, other people and the world throughout the rest of their lives. The parent then needs to match the care to the child's level of development, giving them new experiences and the right level of stimulation, boundaries and feedback for their age and developmental stage. This starts from birth (or even beforehand). Infants need to have their parent's attention and for that parent to be attuned enough to recognise and respond sensitively to the child's feelings.

When I talk about this to parents or carers, they often feel that they fall short of the mark and worry that they need to respond to every signal from the baby correctly the first time and every single time. Actually, the research evidence doesn't show that such perfection is required. From what I've read, I'd say that, provided the baby's basic care needs are met and there is no abuse or harm being caused to them, 'good enough care' equates to understanding the baby's signals and responding to them appropriately at least one third of the time,[2] so most people who worry about this are probably managing it just fine. If you are attempting to help a child catch up for missed experiences, compensate for abuse and/or poor early care and/or changes of placement, and change the patterns they have already formed, then even if you want to be really ambitious this means you should aim to get the message and respond sensitively at least two thirds of the time. That's a lot easier to aim for than 100 per cent, and it means that you can be a great parent even if you are sometimes tired or grouchy or need to do the cooking or go to the toilet rather than interacting with the child at that moment.

There are lots of reasons that a caregiver may not be able to offer attuned care to an infant. As I've already mentioned, they might be physically unavailable because they are simply not around the baby enough for some reason and they leave the child alone (e.g., in their bedroom or in front of the television) or in poor-quality care. It may be that they are constantly multitasking with addictive levels of gambling, internet use, computer games, emails/texts, etc., or they are preoccupied with other stresses in their lives (such as family conflict, domestic violence, harassment, debt, etc.). It may be that they have formed a view that a child is too demanding and have disengaged from them because of their own avoidant templates of how to relate to others. Or they might be emotionally unavailable

---

2   'Good enough' parenting is a legal standard for care that meets a child's basic needs, and doesn't cause them significant harm or expose them to unreasonable risks. It doesn't mean the care has to be perfect. See Hoghughi and Speight (1998), Tronick (1986), Winnicott (1953) and Winnicott (1965).

due to their own mental health or attachment history. They might have physical or sensory disabilities that make it harder to care for a child without support or serious learning disabilities that mean it is harder to recognise the needs of the child. Maybe they are using drugs or alcohol to an extent that means they are unable to offer coherent and consistent care. They might be simply surviving themselves if there is a high level of conflict around or they are in a war zone or living below the poverty line (e.g., as illegal immigrants). The child may have lost a parent to suicide or may have been abandoned or handed round to other members of the family. Each of these scenarios would have a different impact on a child.

☀ Reflection: Your child's experiences

Have a think about what you know of the story that applies to your child or children. Would they have received good-quality care at any point? Would the care have fallen below 'good enough' at any point? What might the experience have been like of growing up in that environment? Don't be surprised if this brings you strong feelings of sadness or anger. These are a sign of your empathy for your child and are important to think about, as they reflect the emotions that the child may need to go through to grieve their losses as they become apparent to them.

Whatever the cause might be, I think it is worth thinking further about what happens when care is not 'good enough'. The first thing that happens is that the child does not get all the right experience bricks for their early development (see Doodle 6). There are gaps where the child should have had the experiences that teach them the components of social skills and provide a positive self-image and resilience. This is something we will come back to. Second, when the child is exposed to a chaotic or threatening environment (such as when caregivers are shouting at each other or intoxicated, or sometimes hurt, mistreat or shout at the baby), this has a huge impact on them, which we will come back to when we think about brain development and the fight-or-flight instinct. The way the body and the brain work and the impact of experience on this will be the subject of the next chapter.

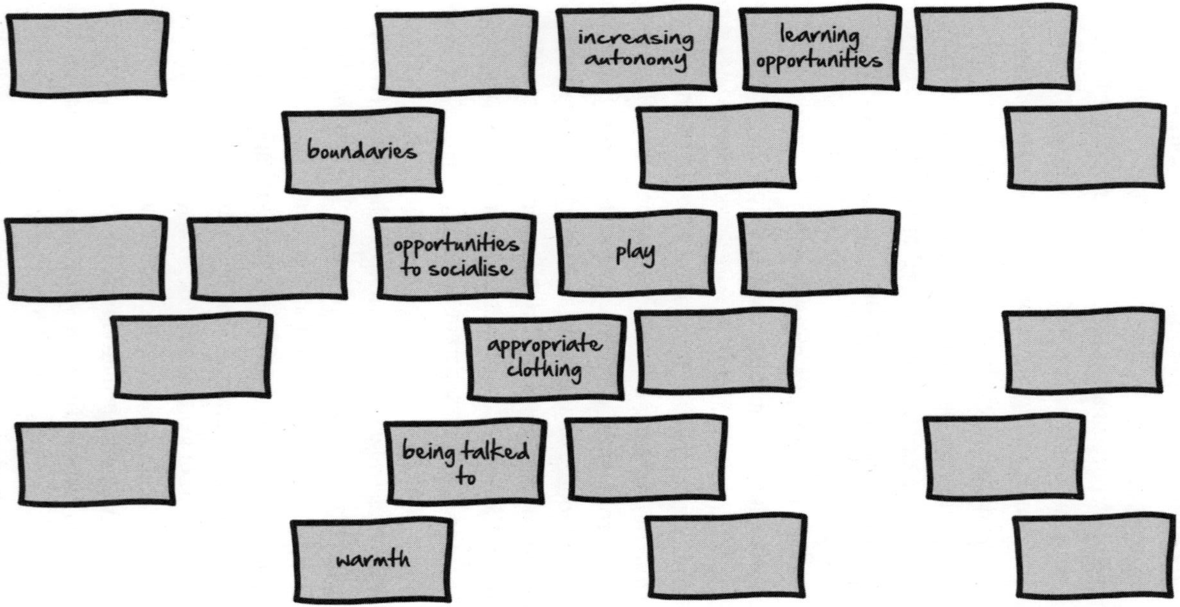

learning opportunities

increasing autonomy

play

opportunities to socialise

appropriate clothing

boundaries

being talked to

warmth

Doodle 6

But first, let's think a little more about attunement and good enough care. When we think about what we would hope that a parent would provide for a child in their day-to-day care, we can list a huge number of things that I see as building blocks for their development. You might want to try this activity (you'll need some paper).

ACTIVITY: BRICK WALLS

Often in my groups I set people the task of writing lists of what good enough parenting looks like for a 0–6-month-old, or a 6–12-month-old, or a pre-schooler, or a primary-school-aged child or an older child. What things will the child have or experience at each age if their care is good enough? These might be as simple as having a safe environment, immunisations, enough sleep, shelter, warmth, healthy food or sufficient hygiene, having someone who will meet their medical needs, change their nappy regularly, smile at them or come when they cry, or experiencing being sung to, being smiled at, physical affection, skin-to-skin contact or being rocked. Those might be some of the things that are applicable for a baby, but for an older child it might be enough stimulation, routine, being listened to, praise, enough structure, opportunities to socialise, being taken to school regularly, being presented in a way that allows them to integrate with their peer group, seeing adults treat each other with respect, being able to learn to negotiate, being rewarded for good behaviour, being treated as an individual and being allowed to gradually develop autonomy.

Each group comes up with lists and then we write each item on a 'brick' of coloured paper (normally a quarter of an A4 sheet). We use these to make a brick wall on the floor of the room with each of these different experiences building up to help the child have healthy development. Groups often think of 50 or more bricks, and when you make a brick wall of all those things, what you get is a visualisation of what makes good enough care. You can arrange it so that, for example, the bottom row of bricks shows the experiences and resources a child should have had at 0–6 months, and then 6–12 months, and then the second year of life, and then the

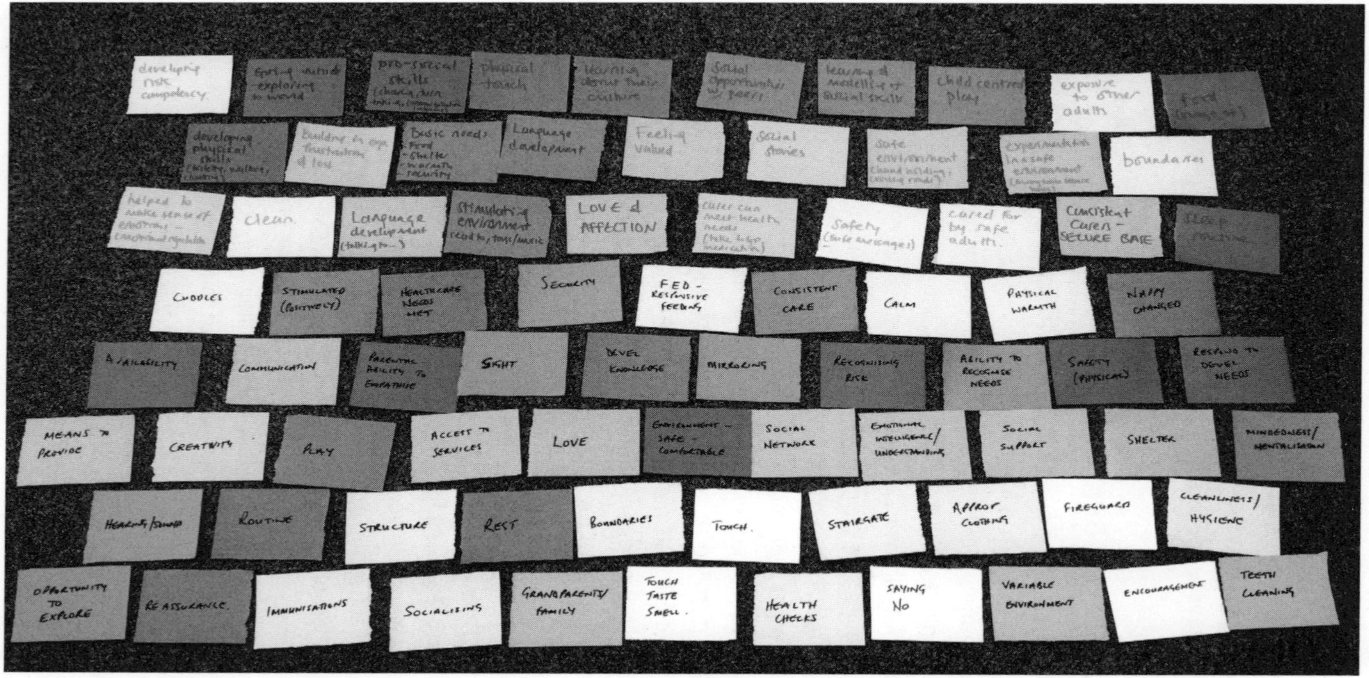

Photograph 1

third year, fourth year and so forth, much like Doodle 5, earlier in this chapter. The result is shown in Photograph 1.

We then consider what is written on each brick compared with the child's real lived experience. Did they have enough healthy food? Would someone have smiled at them? Did they get praise? Was there a routine? We remove each brick where the experience/item was absent. If there wasn't enough of the experience/item, we tear an appropriate amount of the brick off. If there was a skewed version of the experience/item, we turn the brick over or fold or scrunch it up to represent the distorted experience. Photograph 2, a little later in this chapter, shows the typical result of this exercise – many or even most of the bricks are missing or skewed, and the wall doesn't look very strong or safe at all.

Take some time to look at what is left of the wall. Does it look strong? Could you build on top of it? Did you realise so much was missing or broken in the building blocks of the child's life? Does this evoke any feelings for you? People often say these broken walls make them feel sad, or even angry, about what the child has missed out on.

Now think about what it would take to repair the wall. Could missing bricks be replaced, or do you need to help them start building from a lower level or even from the ground upwards? What would this mean for the child? Could you help them to replace missed experiences or do you need to help them catch up with a whole range of developmentally earlier experiences before they can progress with age-appropriate tasks on a solid foundation? Perhaps they need to spend a lot more time with primary caregivers and have very basic needs for nurture met that are normally met at a much earlier age.

If a child is placed with a new family, a foster family or an adoptive family when they are five, the temptation might be to try and build on the layers of bricks relating to a typically developing six-year-old. Now, that would be all very well if all the bricks below were in place, but unfortunately many of the children that we work with have missed out on a lot of those basic and essential experiences. For example, maybe they didn't get enough eye contact, they missed out on smiles, they missed out on routine, they missed out on a healthy diet, they missed out on being praised, nobody wanted to listen to what they had to say and they missed out on having safety. Often when it comes to children who have been removed from their birth families into Care, there are so many different bricks missing from that brick wall that it is a very wobbly wall indeed. So building upwards is not possible until you have filled in the gaps.

I think children are amazing because where there are lots of missed experiences, they will actively seek out the experiences that will fill those gaps. So children who want to be spoon fed, who want to drink from a bottle, who want to come sit on your lap or who play very immaturely are probably doing so to fill a gap in early missed experiences. Once that gap is filled, they no longer have the motivation to seek that missed experience and they move on to more mature things. To try and build more mature behaviour without filling those gaps is building a fragile façade rather than repairing what came before it. Although there may be pressure from school and your social circle to try and get the child to be more age appropriate, this might require skills that are not yet learnt, so it can be more helpful to start at the bottom and work upwards, with attunement and empathy taking priority over academic skills and shaping present behaviour. Quite often, it is really helpful to follow the child's lead and let them have times in their day or in their week where they can act in a more immature way if that is what they need. We sometimes call this 'nurture time'.

Case example: Regrowth

I worked with a boy of about seven when I was training in clinical psychology. His name was Robert and he had been through some really difficult experiences in his early life where his parents were drug users and he was profoundly neglected. When he was in foster care, he asked the foster carer whether he could have a small bear. He would carry this bear around and he called it Baby. He wanted to see how the foster carer would react if he dropped Baby. He wanted to play feeding Baby and putting Baby to bed and looking after Baby and recreating the experiences he had missed in childhood through this small bear. After six or eight months he asked the foster carer if for Christmas he could have a bigger bear that could go in a pushchair. He called that one Big Boy Bear, and after a few months he grew out of that bear as well and was able to be much more age appropriate within the placement.

I was learning about play therapy at the time and in my sessions he went through a parallel process of wanting to role-play being a baby. In some of the early sessions when we were talking about stressful things, he drank from a baby bottle and wrapped himself in a blanket. I should say that I didn't even know there was a baby bottle in that playroom, but he found one and we washed it out so he could suck on it. But just as in the placement, it was simply a phase he was working through. In later sessions he was able to develop more mature behaviour and to start re-enacting experiences with toys and testing out what was okay and not okay about his experiences.

In the group that I run for adoptive and foster parents, making the brick wall is always a really stark visual demonstration of how much is missing from some of these children's lives. Sometimes we build brick walls with 50 bricks and we are left with six or eight bricks when we consider the fostered or adopted children of the parents in the group (see Photograph 2). When I train staff who work in children's residential care homes, sometimes we end up with very small pieces of quite a lot of bricks but no whole bricks at all. It is a strong visual image that lets us realise exactly what the task is of rebuilding those early experiences. When we really think about the child's experiences, we realise that many essential components required for normal, healthy development were missing, that we might otherwise have assumed were present, based on our norms from our own experience in childhood, as parents, or from what we have witnessed in our own social circles. We may not have thought about having these basic experiences as being anything other than

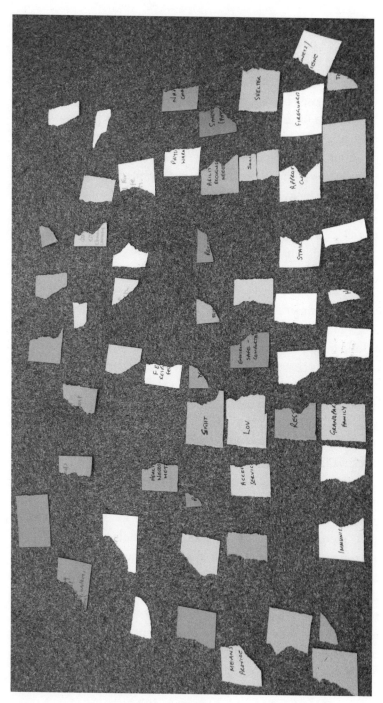

Photograph 2

universal, yet working with children from deprived backgrounds who have experienced abuse and neglect has shown me that many people do not have even the basics required to feel safe, such as safety, shelter, food, cleanliness or parental attention. Recent news stories have talked about how many people live in mouldy homes, the large numbers of families unable to afford food or heating, having to do without sanitary products or basic toiletries, and the resurgence of health conditions related to poor diet, so even in a wealthy country there are many children missing out on basic essentials.

I often encourage foster carers and adoptive parents to really think about what the experiences are that their child missed out on, and how they could let the child gain what was necessary from that experience even now they are much older. If they haven't had the experience of being soothed and rocked as an infant, could they now be taken to play on a see-saw? Could they be tucked into bed at night and have a story read to them or sit on your lap while you are watching television? Each of those things might repair a missing piece of their early experience.

The other thing to say about the wall activity is that some adoptive and foster parents have tried doing it at home with their child. This works particularly well if the child is a bit older, perhaps of secondary-school age. Carers tell me they have replicated the activity and talked with the child about what good care looks like. They have considered what the bricks are that would make up good care at different ages and made the wall with their child, using it as a means to talk about what normal/healthy care is like. Then the child has been able to show what bricks they had or didn't have prior to coming to that placement, which might be the first time they have opened up about some of that information.

Sometimes adoptive and foster parents have been pleasantly surprised by their child wanting to make the wall all over again, this time to look like their current placement, and recognising that there are good things about the care that they are now given. This can be a revelation to the parent, because too often adoptive and foster parents think that the child idealises the birth family and does not recognise that anything is better now than it was before. This activity has proven to be a really non-blaming way of exploring differences in care experiences. Certainly, some of the foster and adoptive parents I have worked with have been really touched by the experience of their child recognising how much better the care is that they are now getting than the care they received in their birth family or in the sequence of placements before they got to their permanent one – particularly if they have always been defensive about their birth family and have never talked about their shortcomings before. That recognition can be quite therapeutic in itself, as of course the more that you reflect on what was missing and what is good about the new placement, the more chance there is that the child will actively be aware of what good enough care looks like. These are important steps towards gaining attachment security themselves.

The earlier the child has suffered trauma, the more emotionally immature they may be. Helping the child needs to occur at their developmental level. The first task is to build up their trust and feeling of safety in the parent or caregiver. Then the carer can mirror the child's feelings using their face, voice and body language, and use a quiet, simple environment to help them become calm. Eye contact can be introduced very gradually. Intimacy can be very frightening for these children. They have learned to survive by not letting other people get too close, as in their experience this could be dangerous, and by not reflecting on other people's thoughts, as this could be too hurtful. Foster carers need to proceed very slowly and gently, as fear will provoke these children to withdraw or become aggressive. They need both playful and caring touch as well as other sensory experiences they may not have had. Even children who have been sexually abused need physical contact and cuddles when they request them or in a gentle and unthreatening way (e.g., putting your hand on their hand or shoulder when they are distressed). Don't demand kisses or hugs from them; let them choose when they are comfortable enough to offer these.

Children may need to learn about how their bodies feel, as they probably had little feedback and help when they were maltreated.

They may keep eating when full or need help to know when they are cold or could put on an extra item of clothing. Some bodily sensations, like a loud noise or the smell of alcohol, can suddenly take them back to traumatic experiences. Recalling these early sensations or traumas can leave children highly anxious and physiologically aroused (ready for fight or flight). They may require 'sensory integration' to help them understand and process sensory stimulation before they can form relationships, talk about their experiences or process their feelings. Children whose world is a confusing mass of sensory information may first need weighted blankets, medication, aromatherapy or massage to help them order and regulate their physiological state before they can cope with sensory integration and sensory stimulation.[3] Only then would they be ready to play out or express their experiences or emotions. After that, it may be possible to give words to their feelings and discuss what has happened to them.

3   See Bhreathnach (2006) and Howe (2005).

CHAPTER 4

Shaping Behaviour

I am sure that most of you have watched *Supernanny* or read books about how to manage children's behaviour with consequences. The general message is to reward good behaviour and to punish bad behaviour so that the child learns to do more of the former and less of the latter. The focus is often on 'time out' or taking away favourite possessions as consequences for unwanted behaviour. The only problem is that these methods rely on the child having a norm of life being nice and having sufficient toys and positive interactions, so that taking these away for a short time is unpleasant but they know they will return. That involves trusting that the relationship is okay and that they are okay (acceptable as a person) even when they get negative consequences.

Being able to learn from feedback depends on many underlying skills that would allow them to control their behaviour and be motivated to achieve the most positive result. A child who has been abused or neglected or has had a chaotic life might not have a secure sense of themselves as a loveable person who is capable of changing their behaviour and succeeding in life. They may feel that any negative feedback is a threat or indicates impending rejection. They may not trust the security of the relationship enough to tolerate feedback like this. They may feel that praise is not sincere or rewards are not deserved, whilst criticism may cut them to the core. They may unwittingly recreate the abuse and neglect they are used to by sabotaging positive outcomes and events and ensuring they gain negative (but familiar) outcomes[1].

However, if you've tried the *Supernanny* route and cancelled all the outings, confiscated their PlayStation and favourite toys and then grounded them for a month, it may have become clear that the system isn't working and you are punishing yourself, as you are going to end up having to work out what to do with a frustrated child for a month! Consequences only work when the child is able and motivated to achieve the positive outcome. As we've seen with the brick-wall activity, many children who come from a background of trauma, abuse and neglect are missing so many basic experiences that they aren't familiar with the idea of a caregiver who cares about them and holds them in positive regard, let alone one who is consistent about what is expected of them and keen to support them to achieve the best possible outcomes. So they might be suspicious of your motivations for being nice or so caught up in survival strategies and accumulating the things that make them feel safe that they haven't reached the stage of forming relationships at all. To parent children like that, we have to adjust the balance of behaviour-management plans so that we focus on building the relationship and making the expectations clear before jumping straight to consequences.

More evidence-based parenting programmes emphasise the importance of the underlying relationship and the need to set any behaviour management techniques on top of the solid grounding of an established loving relationship. In the Incredible Years programme,[2] which is the most well-researched and long-standing programme for managing children's behaviour, they draw a pyramid of the parenting skills that help children to learn best (see Doodle 7). At the bottom, they place the most basic skills like empathy, attention and involvement, play, problem solving, listening and talking. On top of this, they use praise, encouragement, rewards and celebrations to catch the good bits of the child's behaviour.

---

1   See Dan Hughes' (2006a, 2006b) writing on punishment.
2   See Webster-Stratton (2006).

On top of this, they have clear structure, rules and expectations, which are consistently delivered by the parent/caregiver. Then with minor misbehaviour, they ignore, redirect or distract. The use of consequences like 'time out' and loss of privileges are the very tiny tip of the pyramid.

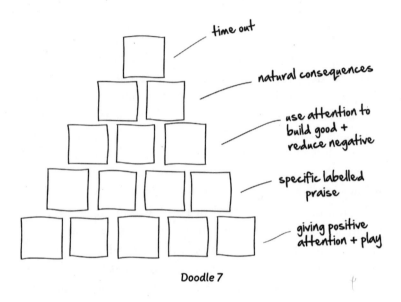

Doodle 7

This focus on building the underlying relationship and focusing on the positives is even more important with children who have experienced trauma, abuse or neglect. The experience of being valued and held in mind is new to them and really core to changing their way of relating to others, and they may never have had a caregiver who will give them positive attention, observe or participate in their play or listen to them, talk about their problems and suggest possible solutions. We will come back to the importance of empathy, and strategies for empathising with older children, in later chapters because I believe it is such an important skill. But this chapter is going to focus on attention and play.

ACTIVITY: GIVING YOUR CHILD YOUR FULL ATTENTION

The challenge is to give your child your full attention for at least ten minutes, three times per week, on a one-to-one basis. You can work out when to fit it in and how to occupy everyone else and explain it to the child. With younger children, you can just say you want to do some fun stuff together. With older children, you might need to say you are practising something you read about in a book and that it might seem a bit strange, or give them some sort of explanation about the purpose of your comments if they respond to them negatively. However, from our role-plays, it is clear that it feels much more uncomfortable to do as an adult, particularly if you are unfamiliar with the technique, than it does to be on the receiving end of this kind of attention as a child.

Find ten minutes in which to give the child your attention whilst they play, do something creative or follow their own interests. It is important to show throughout this time that you are giving your child your full attention and to demonstrate this through body language, facial expression, speech and gesture. Try to follow what the child is doing. Let them lead, do not tell them what to do, try to teach them or ask questions. Only make suggestions if you are invited to or the play/activity has reached an extended pause. Try to show you are observing them by commenting on what they are doing or how they seem to be feeling (e.g., for a young child, 'I see you have picked up the green pen, and you are making lots of big round marks with it and smiling. I think you are enjoying making them'). If they seem to be annoyed by the comments, or question them, make them less frequently or give some explanation. For teenagers, you could ask them to explain a favourite computer game or music track (or talk about a favourite sport, hobby or any other of their interests). You can take the time to notice what they do and what excites them about it, find out how they do it and pay attention to them discussing their topic. So long as the time is interactive, the same goals can be achieved no matter what the activity chosen.

Establish eye contact, move close and smile at the child. If you get a chance, use touch as well as words to show you are close by. If you like what they do, pinpoint what it is you like about their behaviour and be specific in your praise. Don't wait for behaviour to be perfect before praising; praise when it is good for them at that moment. Encourage and praise curiosity, creativity, concentration, patience, persistence, effort.

Don't criticise or structure during your 15 minutes. If the child's behaviour becomes difficult, then ignore it if you can, as if you just happened to look out of the window at that moment, but go back to commenting and praising as soon as there is any small shift towards doing something appropriate. If the child's behaviour degenerates to the point that they are aggressive or out of control, just end the session, but aim to build up a longer session next time. If the session has gone well, tell the child how much you enjoyed it and how you are looking forward to spending time with them again. Make sure what you say is sincere!

Playing with your child like this will build the child's confidence and a positive self-image. It helps to develop independent thinking, self-direction, understanding of others and problem-solving skills. It gives a child a feeling of belonging and being valued. It demonstrates that you are interested in their ideas and actions and respect their views, opinions and how they are feeling. It gives reassurance and a feeling of safety, encouraging them to ask for help if required. It helps to develop their listening skills, patience, sharing and negotiating. Play like this also helps develop children's creativity, social and emotional skills.

NEAR MISSES

In this country, there is a strong culture of telling children what not to do, but it is less common for children to hear what exactly you want them to do. Imagine someone queuing with a child in a bank. It's easy to imagine them being told, 'Don't touch that', 'Don't push', 'Leave the pen alone', 'Don't do that', 'Stop that noise' or any number of negative commands. However, it would probably be more helpful to the child to be told what the parent does want them to do. If a child is told 'We are going to go in the bank and queue now. It's going to be a bit boring waiting to be seen, so I wonder if you can do some quiet games, like counting things that you can see or seeing how long you can stand on one leg', then that child is more likely to be able to succeed at the challenge than one they are not prepared for.

Case example: Learning from feedback

I think back to the process of teaching my husband to drive. I don't think it would have been possible to do it by telling him only what not to do. I'm sure there were one or two moments of 'Don't cross the centre line of the road... no, don't go so near the pavement... don't go so fast when you turn' or similar, but the majority of teaching involved preparing what we were going to do and then giving constructive criticism for what had taken place. I remember lots of preparation conversations like: 'The next thing we are going to do is practise turning right, so when we leave this parking space, you'll take up your normal road position, but get ready to indicate and move the car outward slightly towards the centre of the road so that you end up on the right of our side of the road by the time we reach the give way sign. Do you feel ready to do that?' And when we had undertaken a manoeuvre, we would discuss what went well and what could go better next time, like: 'That was much better than before, I felt like you had more road awareness of the key hazards so I wasn't scared this time, but if you wanted to make it even better you could think about slowing down more gradually ahead of known obstacles like roundabouts.' This strategy of preparation, practice and then feedback is also very helpful for children to learn how to behave.

When you tell them what you want them to do, children can visualise themselves doing it. If you tell them what not to do, they cannot visualise what they should do instead. Worse still, they may imagine themselves doing the wrong thing as you describe the 'don't'. If you say 'When we go to visit your nan, don't touch her china ornaments', then they are only picturing the china ornaments and touching them. It could work better to say, 'When we go to visit your nan, you can play with her stone pebbles and stroke the cat.'

It is also important to make the praise and positive feedback you give both sincere and specific. A generic 'Good boy!' or 'Good girl!' is not as helpful as 'It was lovely to see you give that pen to James when he asked. I really like it when you share so nicely with your brother.' Similarly, gushing praise for something small might feel false, particularly to a young person who has not had much positive feedback in their life. So, they might allow you to say 'Good effort' in a fairly quiet voice but find it uncomfortable or doubt your sincerity if you say, 'You are so fantastic, that was really excellent!' You will need to watch the reaction closely and draw on your experience of this particular child to pitch the feedback at a level they can tolerate and benefit from.

The other opportunity is to capitalise on 'near misses'. So if the child tries to act as you've advised or in a more appropriate way to normal, but this does not go well or is not sustained enough, you can seize the opportunity to praise the effort and recognise the change from the past pattern, but then give feedback about how to be even more successful next time. For example, saying, 'I can see that you tried to be patient with your sister when she started winding you up, and even walked away like we discussed, that's great. Perhaps next time you can come and get me if she follows you, rather than pushing her over?'

When setting targets and consequences, I'd very strongly advocate that a positive focus is the most effective. So on a sticker chart, you must never remove stickers for bad behaviour or have sad-face stickers that are chosen instead of smileys if the target is not achieved. Also, the rewards must be arranged so that each target can be attained and have a meaningful response, as it must always be worth choosing the positive option. For example, if you are working on sharing, with the day broken into seven slots that could each earn a sticker, and you set the target of five stickers in a day earning a consequence (e.g., ice cream after dinner), then if the child misses the first three sticker opportunities in the day, for the rest of the day there is no motivation to comply because no reward is possible. If, however, you offer ice cream in return for five stickers no matter how long they take to earn, then every sticker earned gets them a step closer to the goal. It is also important to set achievable goals and to work on something on which the child is capable of gaining an 'easy win' in a relatively short time to show that you genuinely intend to follow through on the promises made. This will also give both you and the child hope that change is possible.

A favourite technique of mine is to print a picture of something the child wants onto a sheet of stickers and let them gradually assemble the full picture sticker by sticker as a consequence of good behaviour to earn the reward. The picture might be of a new football, the local park (to earn a visit there), pancakes, a book or game they want or the computer (to earn time on it).

When praising your child, remember their emotional level, as you may need to exaggerate the positives as you would for a much younger child. Or you may need to start with very gentle praise and positive experiences so that they are not too overwhelming. Similarly, handling separations needs reassurance with clear demonstrations of joy at reunion as with a much younger child. Remember that children most need to be loved when they seem most unlovable!

Another helpful thing to remember is that disagreements tend to become an argument where each side ups the ante as they go back and forth, with each desiring to assert control over the other or 'win the argument'. A small comment you make to the child might get a snappy response, which might lead you to tell them off, which might lead them to have a tantrum, which might lead you to feel like you need to impose a sanction, which might make them more angry. You can end up going back and forth giving more consequences and making them get more angry until they act out in a more dramatic way or you run out of punishments or recognise things have gone too far. As I mentioned earlier, at its most extreme the child can trigger you to remove all the positive things from their life and end up replicating the neglect that they experienced. Each side is trying to get the last word, and success or compromise becomes more and more unlikely – unless you can break the pattern. Where it is possible, a really helpful strategy is to defuse anger by acknowledging the other person's perspective and any legitimate aspect to their grievance. For example, 'I know it's really frustrating to turn off the telly, but we need to go' is less likely to lead to a negative outcome than 'Turn off the telly, we need to go, otherwise you'll make us late again'.

The other alternative is to opt out of the argument and choose to do something else entirely or give an unexpectedly positive consequence, as this can be a different way to win the battle. For example, if a child is repeatedly difficult in the week leading up to a particular treat or positive experience, there are many parents who would feel that in order to assert some discipline, they should not let the child go. However, many of these children have practised being punished and neglected and missing out on nice experiences many times in their lives but have rarely had the opportunity to experience being rewarded and having positive experiences. So it might be more helpful to comment that the child seems to be acting in a way that leads to punishment but that it's time to change the pattern and go and do something different instead (e.g., an energetic activity, a soothing activity, a snack). For example, it might be that the idea of going to a party or on a holiday is so threatening and feels so undeserved that a child appears to want to sabotage their opportunity to participate by being repeatedly challenging. The parent either continues the pattern of disappointment and rejection or has the opportunity to say to the child, 'You know what, even though it's been a really difficult week and I think the idea is making you a bit anxious, I think it would be a great experience for you to learn how to have more fun, so we are going to go anyway.' Some people worry that this is 'rewarding misbehaviour', a sign of weakness or backing down and feel it is important to 'win' to assert control over the child. However, your ability to choose the outcome the child does not intend or expect is the real show of being the one in control!

Even within discipline you can offer your child choices to give them some control. 'You can carry on shouting and we will leave the shop without buying any shoes or you can be quieter and we will buy shoes – you decide.' Make your rules for behaviour and expectations very clear, spell out the consequences for broken rules and be consistent.

CHAPTER 5

Effects of Parenting on the Infant's Brain

When a baby or toddler is exposed to something frightening or threatening, their internal systems prepare them to protect their safety by using 'fight, flight or freeze' to run away if they are mobile or, if this is not possible, become silent and still to draw less attention to themselves. (The fight part is more prevalent when the child gets older and has the ability to fight back.) If there is continued harm, the infant or child might mentally escape by learning to take their concentration away from the physical sensations that are happening to their body. As adults, we have similar instincts for fight or flight (but normally will only use 'freeze' or mentally escape through dissociation in an utterly overwhelming situation or if we are reminded of a trauma and this is something we have learned as a child).

These responses effectively allow us to escape or defend ourselves when there is danger and are a brilliant survival mechanism. They involve the body sending out chemical messengers called cortisol and adrenaline, which make lots of changes to the pattern of activity in the body and the brain. In the body, the message prioritises blood flow to the muscles and slows down the digestive system (after encouraging us to quickly empty any waste we are carrying – which both lightens the load and deters any predators). We become more active and restless, and notice signs of the changed blood flow, like sweaty palms, a churning stomach and a dry mouth.

In the brain, the amygdala (an almond-shaped bit on the bottom of the horseshoe-shaped section in the primitive central part of the brain called the limbic system) becomes very active, and the prefrontal areas (where we do our most sophisticated thinking, like empathy and understanding cause and effect) become much less active. I have shown where these areas are in Doodle 8. This change in brain activity is very helpful because at times when our safety is at risk, we need to prioritise survival, even when that means not being too sophisticated or logical. That is why you hear stories of people who have done incredible things 'in the heat of the moment', like lifting huge weights or withstanding huge forces to protect their child, because under these extreme stresses the logical part of the brain that would say 'I can't do that' is much less dominant than the part that urges fight or flight, even when this would cause damage to the body or isn't in our long-term best interests.

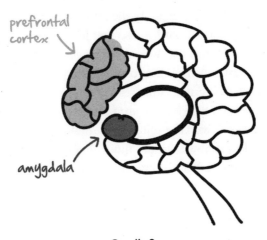

Doodle 8

When an infant is distressed (whether through fear, anger or discomfort), their body and brain go into this fight-or-flight mode until the perceived danger abates. However, they are not very good at differentiating different feelings or distinguishing what is a genuine threat, so that is something they need to learn from the adults around them. One of the things I have always found very interesting is how intuitively most parents help children learn to regulate their levels of physiological arousal (readiness for fight or flight). If you have a baby who is crying, as a parent you will intuitively soothe them by lifting them close to your body and speaking softly to them whilst stroking them. If you have a toddler who is having a tantrum, as a parent you will normally acknowledge that with quite a loud and/or high-pitched voice and large gestures, noting what has caused the distress. You would then pick them up and bring the volume of your voice down to offer some soothing comments and tell them it will be all right as you cradle them in to your body. We often instinctively do what I call the 'jiggle walk', where you lift the baby up and hold them close to you whilst making a motion that bounces slightly to jiggle the baby up and down, patting or stroking them gently on the back. You will then gradually slow the pace of the jiggle and stroke down, using repetitive soothing phrases: 'There there, Mummy/Daddy's here, I've got you, it's okay.' You might stroke them directly on their skin or hair. As the infant calms, you then bring them in more tightly toward you so that it has lots of skin contact and is cuddled in, safe and warm against your body. All of that is very intuitive, so much so that you might never have noticed it.

What most people don't know is that when we are doing that, we are matching their high level of arousal, the fast heartbeat and the fast breathing rate with the volume and rhythm of our movements, and as we slow it down, we are modelling that it is okay for the infant's heart rate and breathing rate to slow down. We are demonstrating non-verbally that the level of physiological arousal they are experiencing is not needed for fight or flight and does not need to remain so high. When we bring a child to our body, the skin-to-skin contact and gentle compression of a cuddle releases oxytocin, a very calming, loving chemical that is involved in a pre-programmed soothing system that overrides cortisol, quietens down the amygdala and lets the child regulate their arousal to a lower level of readiness for fight or flight. When we hold the child so that their head is on our chest or shoulder (which are the most common positions for a cuddle), we are letting the child hear that our heart rate and our breathing rate are not in a highly physiologically aroused state. This allows the child's heart rate and breathing rate to slow down to match. Such co-regulation is instinctive because at a survival level the body is primed to match the arousal level of other people around you. When cuddled against the parent's body, the infant realises at this primitive level that the adult has a greater awareness of potential danger and that the adult does not feel it is necessary to be so physiologically aroused and ready for fight or flight. They are then able to calm themselves to match.

By doing those intuitive things (being attuned to the child and helping them when they are in a state of distress to calm and to regulate), we are teaching children how to activate their soothing systems and moderate their level of physiological arousal. Infants who have this experience of a containing adult learn to gradually recognise and manage their own feelings effectively. Careful research on infant development has shown that you need to learn to co-regulate before you can self-regulate. If a child has not experienced an adult who is able to regulate their level of arousal, and help the child to do likewise, then that child is unable to do anything with their fight-or-flight state except fight or run until the neurochemical messengers run out. No effort of reasoning or consequence will help them to do otherwise, so the key to helping them to learn self-regulation skills is for their carers to model self-regulation and to help the child to recognise, calm and control their emotional states.

Oxytocin is produced at key times in the human lifecycle to reinforce loving relationships. It is triggered by compression, skin-to-skin contact and/or the presence of a loved one. During birth, the child is squeezed through the birth canal, and both mother and child are flooded with oxytocin. It is also produced during skin-to-skin contact and breastfeeding. Hugs feel soothing because the compression and closeness to a loved one trigger it. Cuddles, rocking, massage, holding hands or everyday acts of care like bathing a young child or drying and dressing them can trigger these neurochemicals to reinforce the connection between parent and child. Oxytocin also reinforces romantic and sexual relationships as it is produced at times of intimacy in partner relationships – that is one of the reasons for the stereotype of someone rolling over and falling asleep after sex, as it burns off stress neurochemicals and releases oxytocin that can lower a person's level of readiness for fight or flight. That makes us feel safe and relaxed. During stressful times, like the recent pandemic, finding times for intimacy and/or sexual activity can help to manage anxiety and increase the bond in your relationship. But even in relationships with friends, or between adult family members, or between a person and their pet, touch can be important and soothing. Touch enhances connection, conveys emotion and demonstrates empathy. This level of intimacy was something that people took for granted and really missed during the most restrictive parts of the lockdown. In any form of caring relationship, hugs, holding hands or other forms of gentle touch provide some connection and emotional support, and often convey something at a very basic level about love that is not spoken.

With an infant, touch is used to soothe the child if they are over-aroused (e.g., if the child is distressed or unable to wind down when they need to sleep) and to stimulate them to increase physiological arousal, through tickling or playful interactions (to provide positive experiences and prevent sleep at inappropriate times). It is also used to convey affection and to deepen the connection between caregiver and child, with each releasing the neurochemical reward of oxytocin as they do so. Children who have not experienced physical affection may struggle with physical affection and touch. It may be unfamiliar to experience this level of intimacy, but without it they may not have learnt how to soothe themselves and calm their feelings of fight or flight without having to burn them off through physical exertion or conflict. Finding appropriate ways to use safe touch and to help a child to calm can be a very important step in building trust and helping them to learn to regulate their arousal. This may be very intuitive (e.g., I often find myself reaching out to touch or stroke someone's hand or arm if they are talking about something distressing and I know them well enough for this to feel appropriate) or it may be something you decide intentionally to try. Research shows that humans intuitively recognise the emotional intent conveyed by touch, just as we recognise facial expression or tone of voice. However, we need to be very mindful that, particularly for children who have been sexually abused, touch can feel very threatening and it may be that a side-on hug, or touch to the hand, arm or shoulder, feels less intrusive than face-to-face hugs, sitting on laps or cuddles.

Note: Grooming, sexual abuse or child sexual exploitation can trick the body's system for identifying threat by interacting with the child in a way that triggers oxytocin to be released and lowering the child's fight-or-flight readiness. Using affection, touch, hugs or sexual stimulation can cause the body to override its threat warning system, because oxytocin tells the body to stop producing cortisol and adrenaline. This means that the recipient of grooming or sexual exploitation/abuse may feel safe, or loved, or in control of the situation when this objectively isn't the case, because oxytocin is quietening down their threat alert system, which really should be setting off alarms to warn them about the danger they are in. This explains why so many victims of sexual exploitation perceive the situation irrationally positively when it is happening to them but can perceive the level of risk much more accurately when they see it happening to someone else.

It is worth being mindful of whether the child's arousal level has been 'up-regulated' (trained by early experiences to set a baseline level that is too high for life in a safe environment by being repeatedly exposed to threats, danger or an unpredictable environment) or 'down-regulated' (trained to set a baseline level that is too low by being groomed or sexually abused, or normalised to conflict or threat in their environment so that their body doesn't warn them of risks or they don't react to shouting or violence as if it is out of the ordinary). Either of these can make children and young people react in ways that only make sense if you are aware of the impact of trauma, so this is something we will discuss in more depth in later chapters. The impact of exposure to trauma on the way a child's neurochemistry develops is something that has been increasingly studied over the last two decades, but that research has only led into trauma-informed practice by professionals supporting children and families much more recently. The impact of down-regulation of the fight-or-flight system is probably even less well recognised.

NEUROPSYCHOLOGICAL DEVELOPMENT

We know that babies experience the world at a sensory level, without pattern or meaning. The world seems initially chaotic, but they then start forming patterns and recognising some of the sensory information to be a consistent parent figure. They can then begin to attribute meaning to different experiences. This allows the infant to start developing much more sophisticated functions in the brain, particularly those located in the prefrontal areas. For example, they are able to see events as having a sequence with a beginning, middle and an end. They learn that things have cause-and-effect relationships.

In time, we come to understand the impact of our behaviour on other people and what the consequences are likely to be of different choices. Some of that is the beginning of empathy and the beginning of having a sense that other people experience the world in a way that is similar to us. We start to recognise the difference between thoughts and reality. We begin to label emotions and understand what causes them. We gradually understand that the mental process happens for other people in a similar way to us but they might not have exactly the same thoughts and feelings. We call that 'theory of mind'. Research has shown that a good nurturing and attuned parent helps to develop those skills of cause-and-effect reasoning, empathy and self-monitoring, and theory of mind in an infant, so children who have been through very deprived or chaotic parenting experiences and early life experiences often have difficulties in those areas. Patricia Crittenden[1] suggests that the avoidant child develops their thinking and sacrifices their emotions, and the anxious ambivalent child develops their emotions and sacrifices their thinking.

Creating coherence and meaning is a really important process that normally happens very early in a child's life and is accompanied by structural changes in the brain. When a baby is born, a lot of neurones are in place but they do not have very many connections to the other neurones around them in the brain. Over the course of the first two years of life, it is the connections that grow massively

---

[1] See Crittenden (1997).

in number and help the brain to start linking up ideas, thinking and making much more sense of the world. It is through increasing interaction with the world, having some consistent responses and having consistent people that the child gradually learns to make sense of the world. This search for meaning, achieved through this proliferation of neural connections in the first two years of life, is a really important factor that differentiates the human brain from any other species. There are even researchers who jokingly say a human baby is born two years prematurely, because the connections that are not yet in place at birth for movement, for sensory recognition and for language are all learnt during those first two years.

After the first two years, the connections within the brain that are not used are pruned back. Over the following eight years, until the child is about ten, more connections do grow, but it is harder to repair later the experiences that should have led to connections being formed before you were two and the brain was optimally plastic (in the sense of being able to change and develop). After around the age of ten, when the second round of pruning happens in the brain, it becomes extremely hard to make up for missed experiences, so extended periods of deprivation really have quite a catastrophic effect on the brain. We know from cases of children who have been brought up by wild animals, have survived in really adverse circumstances or have been profoundly neglected and abused that a child who has not been exposed to enough human language before the age of ten rarely develops full language skills. The more profound the absence of experiences is in those first years of life, the harder those deficits are to compensate for later on.[2]

However, research shows that when it comes to early intervention, it is quite an encouraging picture. If you change a child's life experiences before they are two, they can make remarkable change and recovery. In the years between two and ten, they can make significant recovery, and certainly the studies of very maltreated orphans in the eastern European orphanages left by the Ceausescu regime have shown amazing progress, even if there is not usually a

---

2   See Uylings (2006).

total recovery.[3] The effect on the brain from severe neglect is really profound. One thing I have learnt over my career is that the earlier you start to compensate for missed experiences the better. We also know that the earlier maltreatment happened the more impact it has on the brain.

When we think about young children who have been exposed to poor care, the changes are not just at a structural level (in the brain, and nervous and endocrine systems) but also affect how the children function and how they feel. Maltreated children also learn to have different beliefs about themselves, the world and others. (These are the core beliefs or schemas that underlie our way of thinking.) If you have a secure caregiver who gives you attention and positive feedback, and enjoys your company and is stimulating and playful with you, then you learn that you are an okay person, that other people in the world are likely to be okay to you and that the nature of the world and your experiences is likely to be benign and safe. If you have traumatic abusive early experiences then you learn to believe that you are not okay as a person, that there might be something bad or flawed about you, that others will generally treat you badly and are not to be trusted and that the world is a very dangerous and scary place. Those underlying beliefs profoundly impact on the child's self-image, their expectations of relationships and the way they treat others. Interestingly, the beliefs about the self, others and the world formed by not having a secure carer significantly overlap with the type of beliefs and schemas that underlie anxiety and depression and other mental health conditions in adulthood, if they remain unchallenged.

---

3   See Roy, Rutter and Pickles (2004).

CHAPTER 6

Through the Generations

A parent is your first model of relationships and the resource that equips a child for life. I like to think about it using the image of balloons,[1] which are shown in Doodle 9. If you imagine a parent as a balloon, their job is to inflate the baby balloon with enough air to float into the world of good relationships and to be able to cope with the challenges and knocks of life. An effective attuned parent is able to use their own resources to fill the balloon and to protect it and help it become independent by tying a knot to hold in the air. The parent is 'internalised' by the child, who can draw on their skills and experience to become an on-board puncture repair kit in times of stress. The child balloon can continue to inflate itself internally and through other healthy relationships and is both resilient and able to float up to where other healthy balloons are, where it can form relationships. If a parent does not have many emotional resources, then their balloon is not effectively filled and it will struggle to fill up the child. They might see the child as a potential source of air, rather than recognising how much of their own air will be required to inflate it. Or they might remain mouth-to-mouth with the infant balloon, as they do not know how to separate or provide the tying off that will keep the air inside. Or the child might be exposed to a very prickly and hazardous environment that damages it before it can even be fully inflated. The baby balloon is unable to internalise that 'puncture repair kit' and therefore easily punctures under stress. So,

---

1   With thanks to colleagues from Action for Children in Scunthorpe who introduced me to this metaphor for Object Relations during a workshop on building self-esteem in 1999.

without another balloon constantly inflating it, the balloon easily sinks to the ground amongst other punctured balloons and the risks of many prickly obstacles (and some low-floating predator balloons which seem to offer the much-needed air but at the cost of additional punctures that cause more air to escape in the long term).

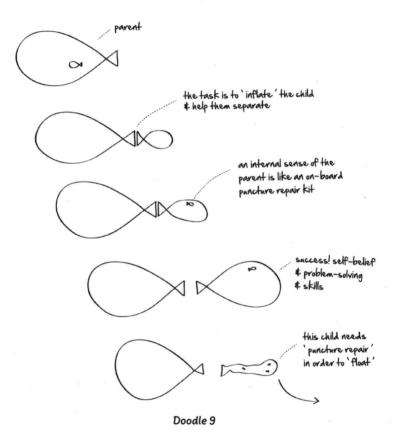

Doodle 9

Many carers tell me how exhausting it is to constantly try to inflate a 'leaky balloon' of a child and how it takes up all their own air (as well as how vigilant they have to be for hazards and predators in the environment as the child gets older). So my task as a therapist in this metaphor has always been to attempt to help parents (with additional tools and knowledge, and perhaps some of my own air at times) to inflate and tie off the balloon of their child, or to complete puncture repairs, or to work with young people or adults to repair their own puncture wounds, recognise risks and predators, and create their own puncture repair kit to enable them to float higher in their future lives and relationships.

Doodle 10 illustrates how patterns of attachment transmit through the generations. This is something we have already touched on, and it might be self-evident from the balloon doodle that a parent with limited emotional resources is not always well equipped to set up their child with those emotional resources. However, I think it is worth mapping it out a bit more and then thinking about how adoption and fostering (or other changes of placement) affect things.

As I hope you will have gathered by now, you need a certain level of internal security to hold your child in mind (that is, to consistently consider their experiences and feelings) and create the kind of predictable and nurturing life experience for a child to develop optimally and have a secure attachment. A parent who is able to hold the child in mind can then teach the infant to recognise and regulate their emotions, to have empathy and to have good social and negotiating skills. There will often be times that the child will see or experience the adults in their life showing empathy (e.g., asking someone else how they are feeling or how their day has been; checking if someone is feeling tired or unwell, or has injured themselves), social skills (like offering hospitality to guests, telephoning or video-calling friends or relatives), and regulating their emotions (e.g., dealing with a frustrating scenario without losing control, getting slightly angry but calming down and retaining the relationship).

They might also be explicitly taught these skills by adults interacting with them in particular forms of play or interaction. For example, we often have toy telephones or tea sets for preschool children. Playing with the phone, we teach children to say hello, to find out who they are speaking to and to ask the other person how they are. We then share information that the other party may not yet know. So it teaches about how each person has different knowledge, experiences and preferences. Playing with a tea set, we encourage children to ask about other people's desires and preferences ('Would you like a cup of tea? Do you take milk? Sugar? Do you want some cake? Did you like the tea?') and we try to change up the pattern to expand their repertoire. With dolls or figures, we often ask questions about their inner world ('Is dolly sleepy? Does bear like his sandwich? You'll make penguin dizzy if you keep swinging him round like that'). As children get older, we ask them about their day at school or their preferred activities. We discuss interactions with teachers or friends – especially ones that have not gone well. Even with video games, we might ask about a character's goal or motivations ('Who are you playing? Where does he want to get to? What are his powers? Is he a goodie?'). Each of these interactions teaches the child about the social world and how to engage with other people. They learn about different people having different thoughts, feelings and preferences and begin to learn how to judge if their motivations are benign or harmful. If we do our preparation well, that infant will be able to connect with more socially appropriate peers. They will learn all the positive social skills that will help them be successful in life (we call these pro-social skills). I tend to say that if they learn these skills they can 'play the tea-and-cake game' as a short-hand for having the building blocks in place for early pro-social skills.

If you picture a nursery, there is often a kitchen corner where well-adjusted children very often will play games of making people food and drinks. If one starts playing, then other children will recognise that game and know how to join in. So if you put a set of three- or four-year-olds together, they often play at making each other cake, making each other tea or cooking other familiar food for each other. When offered play food by another child, they will say 'Oh what a lovely drink of tea, thank you very much' and they will have that kind of rehearsed social hospitality embedded in their play. A child who has learnt all of those good pro-social skills will make friends with others who have those good pro-social skills. Whereas if in that nursery there was a child who had been exposed to a very different kind of lifestyle, they might not know how to play those tea-and-cake games, because that might not have been the lifestyle they experienced or something that was taught to them.

Let's imagine the play of a child who has been brought up in a house where they were profoundly neglected by parents who mis-used alcohol. A child in those circumstances might re-enact their life in the home corner in a very different way. They might even sit down on a chair and slouch back and say, 'Oi bitch, bring me a beer.' Now, if someone else in that room has had a lifestyle like that, they might know how to play that game, they might know how to interact to play out the experiences that they have had in their family circumstances. So children with similar experiences are drawn together. And when you have children as young as three or four who are already socially grouping according to the kind of parenting experiences they have had, it is no surprise that people go on to form their later relationships with people with similar attach-ment experiences, because just as the children have common play, they have common language and reference points, and common expectations of how relationships work.

This is reinforced by the fact that if you come from a very high-emotion household where you have had to be ready for fight or flight at all times, the very well-behaved children will seem boring and dull (and maybe a bit too saccharine sweet to trust), whereas the kids who are getting into lots of trouble will be a better match for your level of physiological arousal and might seem a lot more authentic and follow familiar patterns of behaviour. Children like this will have very sensitive threat systems within their brain but very under-developed soothing systems.[2] This means that they seek out excitement, conflict and activity; they are neurochemically matched to all the adrenaline that goes with the excitement. So, for a number of reasons, people group with people who have got similar background experiences.

⛯ Reflection: Spotting patterns

Have a think about your own social network. How similar are your friends' attachment patterns to your own? Maybe they have been through different life experiences, but are their beliefs about

---

2   See Cozolino (2002).

parenting and the nature of their relationships similar? Even without having asked too much about people's backgrounds, we often associate with people with similar attachment patterns to ourselves and pass on our own experiences through the generations. Many parents report being surprised to hear their parent's voice coming out of their own mouths to their children or otherwise re-enacting experiences that they had long forgotten.

For example, it might be that most of your friends are in long-term relationships that are successful, and where there is divorce and separation it is handled in a fairly amicable way. Or it might be that most of your friends chop and change relationships and have lots of fights and fallings out with each other. Likewise, it might be that your friends talk about thoughts and feelings, or it might be that they are very guarded and view those things as personal, so they keep conversations very superficial.

These clusters of similar patterns also pass on from parent to child. I think about that in terms of the patterns that pass from one generation to another (which we call transgenerational cycles). What happens is that a parent who holds the child in mind and offers secure and attuned care creates a healthy pattern for the child (see Doodle 10). They are able to protect the child from harm and soothe them when they are distressed. This high-quality care teaches the infant how to recognise their feelings, to regulate and soothe them when they become physiologically aroused, to link cause and effect and to read others with effective empathy – important components of social skills. The parent reflects how much they enjoy and value the baby, so the child learns that they are valuable and loveable. They gain their identity and self-image within the positive mirror of the parent's experience of them. They learn that other people are reliable and sensitive and that the world is mostly safe and benevolent. If another child is repeatedly mean or hurts them, they tell a trusted adult who can advise and support them to seek out different friends.

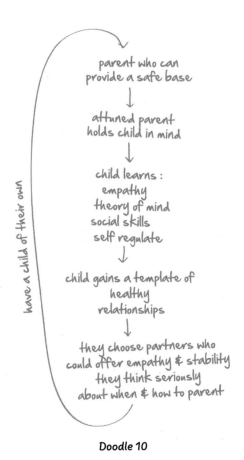

parent who can
provide a safe base

↓

attuned parent
holds child in mind

↓

child learns :
empathy
theory of mind
social skills
self regulate

↓

child gains a template of
healthy
relationships

↓

they choose partners who
could offer empathy & stability
they think seriously
about when & how to parent

have a child of their own

Doodle 10

The infant learns the building blocks of how to form healthy relationships, and as that child gets older, some of those healthy relationships go on to be romantic relationships. The young person then tests out the relationship to see if it feels 'right', using the standard of what they are familiar with and the way they expect to be treated, and will pick the most positive relationship to commit to in the longer term. A young person with insight about the importance and demands of parenting then tends to take quite seriously the prospect of having a child themselves, so they plan (as best they can) the time at which they would want to have a child. They would typically decide to do that within the context of a healthy relationship or with a good support network around them, and so when they become a parent, they have the capacity to hold that child in mind and the cycle can repeat itself. If there is an unplanned pregnancy, they draw in support and make an informed choice about whether they are ready and able to be a parent. They then work hard, with the support of their network, to create the safety and stability that the baby will require.

In the cycle of what happens in a child when the parent does not have the capacity to hold them in mind, the picture is quite different (see Doodle 11). Here, the parent is chaotic, perhaps unavailable, unpredictable or even harmful at times. This means that the child is placed in a situation where their innate threat system is triggered. To compound this, they are not soothed sufficiently, and the parent does not teach them to regulate their arousal. The parent is in 'survival mode', where they don't have the emotional capacity to consider the baby's experience beyond providing basic care, and even that might vary according to other stressors such as domestic violence, their mental health or substance abuse. So the infant does not learn those skills about empathy and to link cause and effect; they just learn from the mirror of their carer that they are unworthy of love – or if the parent is physically or emotionally abusive, that they are a bad child and deserve maltreatment. The infant gains poor self-image and beliefs that others and the world are dangerous, critical or unreliable.

The developing infant does not gain those social skills that the child in the previous family learnt. They are primed for threat and maintain quite high arousal. This child goes on to be the young person who takes risks and may be more aggressive, or they might be withdrawn and aloof. They may play the games that are very exciting or dramatic and get involved in conflict, for example through bullying or being bullied. They may play the 'beer game' instead of the tea-and-cake game and form exciting but dysfunctional relationships. They are more willing to take risks and experiment with drugs and alcohol (which might feel rewarding if they reduce anxiety or blur traumatic memories). As the child becomes an adult and those dysfunctional relationships become sexual, they often become pregnant in an unplanned way. This means that a baby might arrive to a teenage parent, and/or without much planning, and in the context of relationships that are not very healthy, characterised by parental conflict and/or substance abuse. They may go on to parent that child without appropriate support or in a dysfunctional relationship, and the baby experiences a parent who is in a chaotic state and repeats that cycle. There is also a subgroup of neglected and maltreated adolescent girls who believe that having a baby will be their own special relationship that will be a source of unconditional love and make them feel valued. This then forms a mismatch with the reality of having a baby, which (in the early months at least) is often an exhausting set of continual demands and can lead to enormous stress and feelings of inadequacy, whilst your hormones adjust to parenthood. Without a supportive partner and/or a good support network, the tasks of parenting can feel overwhelming. Postnatal depression can further compound this and make it even harder to parent. The sad reality is that those who are most driven to fill the love gap in their life with a baby are often the least well equipped to meet the needs of that baby, and unless they are given sufficient support they can end up having negative experiences of parenting that might unwittingly replicate the issues that they themselves experienced. At worst, they may also end up with the trauma of being judged to be an inadequate parent and having that child removed from their care, further adding to their distress and shame. For this reason, I would always encourage girls who have experienced trauma and poor early care to delay parenthood for as long as possible (certainly until they have a healthy relationship and a network of support and have processed their own experiences), and to use reliable long-term contraceptive methods to do so.

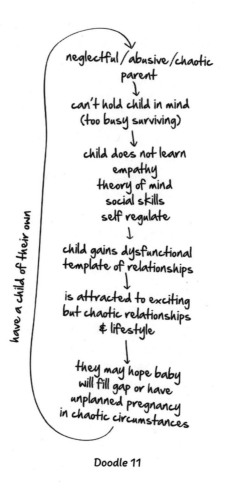

Doodle 11

PATTERNS THROUGH THE GENERATIONS

It is worth thinking about the patterns that we ourselves come from and those that our children have experienced. It is not always as polarised as the two extremes described above, but it might be that traits you thought were passed down through the genes or because of some kind of organic disorder the child was born with could in fact be the product of their parenting experience. The study of epigenetics is beginning to shed light on these differentiations. It looks as if there might be some children who are resilient genetically (like dandelions, which can grow regardless of the environment) but others who are more vulnerable and sensitive to the environment (like orchids, which need certain conditions to thrive). We will come back to considering the superficial similarities between children who have been exposed to poor early care and have damaged attachment templates with the traits associated with some common diagnoses in Chapter 10.

After reading about attachment patterns that transmit through generations and can stay entrenched for a long time or become healthier through a change of placement, you might be wondering about change in the opposite direction. What about people who are in a good pattern but then end up going through so many stressors they move onto a more negative track, for example due to a destructive relationship? The first thing to say is that having had a sound footing in secure attachment relationships is very powerful – children who get good care in their first couple of years tend to make quicker recoveries and do better overall, even when they experience abuse, neglect and chaotic care, than those who lack that initial foundation. In the same way, one secure attachment relationship, even if it is not with a primary carer, can also provide resilience. It is also worth saying that attachment styles are quite stable, and it takes a fairly major event or accumulation of events to significantly change how a person's attachment style functions.

However, there are some people who go on to be a parent and then face lots and lots of stresses, which will inevitably impact on their parenting (e.g., if they live in a war zone or have a very destructive relationship, they are seriously injured or unwell or they have a mental health break down). As I mentioned, bereavements and losses (e.g., pregnancy loss or unsuccessful IVF) and other life stressors can push people temporarily from the secure attachment zone into insecure but organised styles of interacting with others. However, over time these will typically revert back to the secure attachment style that is more familiar. Hopefully, securely attached adults form healthy relationships with others who are securely attached and so choose good partners and a supportive network, but our life experiences can change. For example, you can get into a relationship that becomes progressively worse until it becomes so destructive that you become less and less secure. Having had a secure attachment helps people to recognise the shortcomings of such relationships and the need to protect the children, but life is not as simple as that, and children are sometimes exposed to stresses even by parents who had good childhoods themselves.

However, if those parents have had the background experiences of being parented effectively, then a lot of their intuitive responses are probably still protective even though their lifestyle is chaotic due to factors outside of their control. Plus they are more likely to have good sources of social support to prop them up when they are under stress. The experience of having a parent who is temporarily under stress generally turns out to be less damaging for the children than if they have come from a background in which they have become accustomed to incredibly chaotic situations and simply don't recognise the risk or the harm that is being done. But, of course, this varies from situation to situation and person to person, because there are so many different variables at play.

The interesting thing about trauma is that there is a dose effect.[3] The more you are exposed to trauma, the more people who are involved in that trauma or perpetrating harm and the longer you are exposed to it, the more impact it has on the child. Normally, stressors that a parent with a healthy template will be dealing with tend to have a much milder impact on the child than a chronic pattern of dysfunction that is repeated through a sequence of similar dysfunctional relationships, or due to chronic substance misuse or being passed around a family. Similarly, we know that children do better when they are removed earlier and reach permanence (a family placement intended to last until adulthood, such as adoption or long-term fostering) without too many changes of placement in the interim.

It is a sad indictment of the current lack of placement choices and training/support for foster carers that we are not always able to provide such a pathway and that children may be removed and rehabilitated back to the birth family several times before being

---

3   See Read *et al.* (2005).

permanently removed, or they may go through a series of short-term placements before finding their 'forever family'. Even then, not every placement runs smoothly, and there appears to be a lack of accessible and skilled support when problems begin to appear. There is currently a major problem with achieving permanence for children aged over seven because of the lack of availability of long-term placements. Sadly, because of the lack of choice, the placements are not always ideally matched to the child, and some carers are encouraged (either for financial reasons or due to the demand for placements) to take on more children rather than being able to focus on just one. And, of course, every placement that comes to an unplanned ending worsens the prognosis of the child.

CHAPTER 7

Changing Patterns
The Tug of War of Attachment

Whilst we are considering what happens across the generations, an interesting thing for social workers and adoptive and foster parents to think about is the fact that, in broad brushstrokes, we are trying to move a child from the unhealthy transgenerational pattern into the healthy transgenerational pattern (see Doodle 12). With a real-life family that you are involved with, it is often very difficult to know when you should intervene, unless there is a single terrible incident that becomes a catalyst for intervention. However, to me, this really highlights the importance of decisive early action, because if you can fix the problem then the child can stay in their family of origin without lasting negative impact, and if you remove that child very early then better placement options are available to them. Within these they can learn empathy, self-regulation and pro-social skills, and may be able to go on to form healthy relationships themselves. If you leave it too late, then the child may have already developed some quite entrenched patterns of forming dysfunctional relationships, and that work becomes harder.

Some people suggest that this means the main focus of intervention and the deadline for adoption should be in relation to babies and infants under two years of age. However, although these children do the best when placed into alternative families, there is good evidence that children under five generally thrive in new homes, with fewer than 5 per cent of placements 'disrupting' (breaking down after the match is made). In fact, the majority of children

placed with high-quality carers and appropriate professional support can still be successful in permanent new homes even when
they are six, seven or eight years old. Permanence is successfully
achieved with certain types of children and certain types of carer
even into adolescence. So, in my view, aiming for permanent placement within a family wherever possible is still worthwhile, because
it can change the pattern for generations to come. With adolescents,
even if the change in attachment style does not happen fully within
one generation, there are still improvements in that child's quality
of life, and intervention can also make positive impacts on the next
generation. That is because those children then go on to be more
likely to become earned secure and to offer more attachment security for their children than they would have done if they had stayed
in the very chaotic life within their birth family.

Doodle 12

Professor Marinus van IJzendoorn did an analysis of all the studies[1] of the outcomes of adoption. He describes adoption as being the most powerful intervention ever studied and as being more effective at changing the long-term results for children than aspirin is at reducing pain. His research shows us that the outcomes of children adopted early enough change from those of the deprived, abusive and chaotic pathways into which they were born to being the same as would statistically be expected of the birth children of adoptive families. They gain in all kinds of outcomes, including IQ.

I believe the outcomes are so remarkable because adoption takes children out of chaotic, socially deprived families and puts them into families that are very committed to the acts of parenting – those who have chosen to do parenting for a living in the case of foster care or who have desperately wanted a child and have thought about it a great deal in the case of adoptive parents. This means that the people who adopt or offer other forms of permanence to children are generally the people who can hold a child in mind, and they tend to be in less chaotic, slightly better socio-economic circumstances with less stressors than the birth families.

Van IJzendoorn's studies show us that adoption works brilliantly before the child is two. Other data tells us that you can be pretty optimistic about adoption before the child is five. But sadly, the further the child goes beyond five, the more risk there is that the patterns are entrenched and that the placement will not last them until adulthood. By the time the child is nine, around half of all placements intended to last until adulthood break down. One of the tasks of professionals is to recognise the need to intervene decisively and early, because that can mean a difference of a generation in how fast we change these patterns. However, the data is incomplete at the moment, because there are limited studies following up children who are adopted later that explore the factors related to risk and resilience and the impact of providing the right packages of support

---

1   This process of compiling all the data from multiple studies is called a meta-analysis.

for those whose placements are the most risky because of the age and experiences of the child.

I find it helpful to think about what happens to a child's attachment style in a placement and the impact they have on the people around them with the image of a tug of war (see Doodle 13). Whether children change their attachment pattern or not is about the balance between competing forces: the parents trying to make the child more secure and the child trying to make everyone else less secure (though the latter is not a conscious or deliberate process). Typically, the tug of war happens when a child who is from an insecure attachment pattern gets placed into a new family who are not used to that pattern.

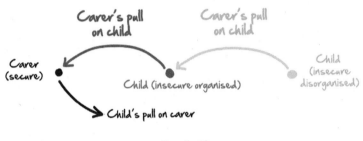

Doodle 13

Let's assume, for the sake of Doodle 14, that the child is placed with a family who are in the secure category. Let's first consider what happens if a child who is one of the organised but insecure categories is placed in that family. In that scenario, there is a tug of war in attachment styles: the child's behaviour and way of behaving and relating to others encourages the carers to become less secure, and the carers' way of behaving and relating encourages the child to be more secure. Each of them is familiar with the patterns that happen in their own backgrounds and behaves according to their own patterns learnt from their own life, and each finds the other's patterns a bit disconcerting and unfamiliar. Perhaps the child perceives the household as too quiet and is only used to calm periods when they're short intervals that precede a storm, so they learn to provoke the storm to get it over and done with and to burn off that fight-or-flight chemistry they are used to producing in their body and brain. The parents, on the other hand, are used to a nice quiet life and experience the child as constantly misbehaving and provoking needless conflict. We'll come back to patterns of physiological arousal (readiness for fight or flight) in the next chapter. The point here is that there is a mismatch.

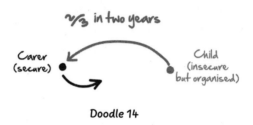

Doodle 14

But let's think about that tug of war a little more in the context of some of the research that tells us about placement outcomes, particularly some studies done by the Coram group[2] using play-based assessments at different periods of time after adoption. If a child who is insecure but organised is placed with carers who are secure, the pull on the carers is to make them react in ways that are less secure and more familiar to the child. The child's behaviour causes stress that can put pressure on the parents and make them react in more disorganised ways. Meanwhile, the parents' consistent and loving responses can help the child to challenge their norms and see more pro-social role models. The pull on the child is that these carers are doing things differently and are reacting in a way that creates a secure base and gives them the opportunity to learn that way of behaving and over time developing a more secure attachment template. If the carers can stay in that secure position (which is something that we will come back to below), then the research tells us that two thirds of the time in a two-year period, they win that tug of war and the child becomes secure. That is an amazing outcome and shows the power of living within a new family. I find the Coram

---

2   See Kaniuk, Steele and Hodges (2004).

group follow-up studies quite encouraging in terms of who wins that tug of war.

If you have a child who is insecure disorganised, it is as if they are a step further away from that secure pattern that you need to create, so the tug of war that happens is more intense (see Doodle 15). These children make a much stronger pull on the carer to disorganise and become less secure and that puts pressure on the carer's relationships and on the placement, which is more at risk of breaking down. However, if the carer can remain secure, that child will gradually become more organised in their attachment style. The research suggests that two thirds of the time in a two-year period they will reach a position of being organised insecure (the middle attachment category and point in the doodle) and they are just as likely over the following two years to continue to become secure.

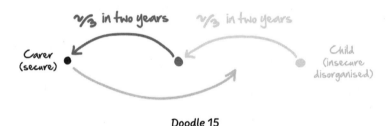

Doodle 15

Doodle 15 is a fairly optimistic diagram, but it does beg the question of what happens to the one third of kids who get stuck in their disorganised pattern (at the far right of the diagram) and the one third of kids who get stuck in the organised insecure position (in the middle of the diagram). Well, I think two things happen. One is that, despite their best intentions, the new parents do not always provide a secure base or are not always able to sustain that. Although adoptive parents and foster carers are selected because of their ability to provide a healthy attachment relationship and good quality of care, I know that it is not always the case that they are in the optimal secure category at all times. This is particularly the case with adoptive parents, who have often been through a lot of quite traumatic experiences in their own lives and stressful experiences of fertility treatment, lost pregnancies or relationship breakdowns. For a significant proportion of adopters, the very fact of having to accept an adoption as a means to have a child, rather than having a birth child, is a huge psychological challenge. There is then a long stressful process of being approved, and there may often be compromises from their image of a newborn baby to the reality of adopting a child from the Care system with a complex history. Whatever the story that has led them to adoption, the process often contains pressures that bring them out of the secure category themselves or make them more vulnerable to the challenges that the children bring.

There is a different but equally interesting pattern that applies to foster carers, who have often chosen to be carers as a career and had to make compromises and sacrifices with their lifestyle and the impact of foster children on their birth children and relationships. Children they care about may be moved on to other placements or rehabilitated back to a birth family (even where this may not appear to the carer to be in the child's best interest), or they may require a certain number of children in placement to make ends meet. The amount of support available is variable, and so are the needs of the different children who are placed. Foster carers themselves, interestingly enough, are quite often in the 'earned secure' category; they have often been shaped by childhood experiences that are not ideal, but because they have become very resilient, they are motivated to pass on some of that resilience to the children who are placed with them.

As a result of these multiple stressors at play in the parents, the attachment patterns the children bring can seem to amplify small manageable sources of stress into bigger issues. Some placements break down. Some couples split up. In some placements, the stress brings out unhelpful patterns in the parent that they didn't know existed or thought were resolved. Sometimes carers see themselves behaving in ways that they are not very comfortable with and start to doubt their ability to parent. When that happens, they are not able to sustain their secure patterns as a way of looking after that child. That is one of the things that we will come back to in Chapter 18, because it is really important to maintain those healthy patterns against the child's disorganised pull in the tug of war. This might involve using what I call your tag team, the people who can take over from you and give you a break for support (as in team wrestling) when you are getting sucked in.

When considering why it is that some children get stuck and parents do not always win the tug of war, part of the difficulty is that sometimes carers themselves are unable to maintain a secure base. I also think that when you place sibling groups together, they can reinforce the familiar level of emotional volume and attachment style between themselves, so it becomes harder for carers to change the children's behaviour. I acknowledge that there are big advantages in keeping siblings together for other reasons, like their identity and to avoid any further loss of attachment figures, and understand why this is considered positively by social services and the legal system. However, I think that when you place large sibling groups together, you need to be a little wary, especially if you believe the children involved have an insecure disorganised attachment style. In my experience, the larger the group of siblings, the stronger the pull is towards maintaining their attachment style, the slower the journey is towards the adoptive or foster carers' attachment style and the higher the risk of placement breakdown or long-term difficulties within the placement.

The second challenge is that even when parents are able to make a secure base, there are some children who remain stuck in the disorganised insecure category and seem to resist the pull towards organising their attachment pattern. In my experience, those young people get stuck there either because they are so dysregulated in terms of their arousal (their emotions are out of control) that they are unable to be in a state where the right parts of their brain are active, or they resist the kind of nurture that would help them to change. These children can also be so aloof that parents find it hard to build a relationship with them, or they are so chaotic that it becomes extremely hard to be an active and nurturing parent, and the placement is at much greater risk of breaking down. This is more likely to be the case if they have experienced very severe or very early trauma.

When children get stuck and don't seem to be organising their attachment pattern at all within the first 12 months in placement, I would really think about requesting specialist input from local services. This might include getting a referral to the local Child and Adolescent Mental Health Service (CAMHS), where a psychiatrist could consider whether medication would be a helpful part of that package, and maybe a clinical psychologist or specialist therapist could consider the type of therapy that would support the family further. Getting help at the right time is critical, because I think if you are stuck in the disorganised category and that pattern is not changing, it becomes increasingly risky over time that the placement will not be sustained. Placement disruptions (a polite term for placements that end in an unplanned way) are really damaging both for the children and for the adults who care about them and have tried to offer them a home. Preventing placement breakdown in the high-risk groups is where services need to target most support.

When considering the tug of war of attachment, it is also worth commenting on the importance of self-care and getting the right support for foster and adoptive carers. This is essential, because as a foster or adoptive carer, it is your support network and your professional network who can help anchor you in that secure position. If you are feeling like you are in it alone and that this tug of war is dragging you in, you really need to bolster up that support network, because it is not a job that one person (or even a couple) can do in isolation.

I believe very strongly that we should be recruiting a wide variety of adopters and foster carers. This should include single people, couples and other family configurations (e.g., an adult alongside their parent/s) and should include people from different socio-economic groups, ethnicities, lifestyles, genders, sexualities and ages. In fact, I believe all a child needs is one or more people who will love them, value them as an individual and put their needs first. However, to do this more demanding version of parenting (which is in itself the most challenging job most people will ever undertake) effectively and remain healthy and resilient with sense of humour intact, that person or people will need a considerable support network to draw on. Neither adoption nor fostering are a one-person job, so you need to think about where you get that support from. This is even more important the further to the right in Doodle 15 the child is when they are placed with you, because the more people with positive secure attachment styles who are around, the more modelling of that attachment style the child experiences. And the carer is also reinforced in their own healthy patterns and is less likely to be sucked into the unhealthy patterns that the child has brought with them from their past.

This book, and the groups I run, are all about helping parents and carers feel skilled and supported in the challenge of parenting children who have experienced poor early care, trauma, neglect and/ or abuse to increase the chance that placements have a positive outcome. This information and support is intended to help parents and carers to make sense of the challenges the child brings into their home and to maximise the impact that the parent or carer can have on the child's attachment template.

CHALLENGE: ACTIVELY CHALLENGING YOUR CHILD'S ATTACHMENT TEMPLATE

Part of making the best impact in re-parenting your child comes from recognising and actively challenging your child's unhealthy attachment patterns, learnt from poor early care. Research following up the Coram study that I referred to earlier shows that when foster and adoptive carers are more aware of their child's attachment pattern, and challenge it more overtly, the child's attachment pattern changes more quickly towards a more secure pattern. Thus, it is very helpful if you are able to recognise the pattern your child is showing and then apply particular techniques.

- Avoidant children, whose parents were anxious or rejecting when they made emotional demands, learn to exclude their own dependency needs and become self-sufficient and emotionally self-contained. Displays of need or vulnerability in others or dependency feelings in themselves can make them feel anxious and avoidant. The challenge for their carers is to find a way to offer the nurture and reassurance that these overly independent children need, and to help them to access and understand their feelings, especially those involving dependency and vulnerability.

- Ambivalent children, whose parents were insensitive, have learned to increase their demands and show distress to gain a response. They are desperately worried about being ignored or left alone and not having their needs met. They appear angry, dissatisfied or provocative in relationships but also defer to others and ignore their own thoughts or behaviour. The challenge for carers is to help the children feel loved and valued but also understand their own relationships and behaviour, gain a greater sense of self and autonomy and to be content enough to tolerate separation.

- Disorganised children do not know how to react, as their parents have been the source of their fears and abuse while also being their supposed source of care and support. It is very difficult for children to learn to regulate their emotions when faced with unpredictable danger and inconsistent care. They have confused expectations of relationships and may only feel safe when they are in control of others and their feelings and needs are denied. The challenge for their parents or carers is even greater: to help them to feel safe with a caregiver, to learn about healthy relationships and to acknowledge their own feelings. They will also need to learn about how to read other people's thoughts and feelings, and to regulate their own emotions and level of readiness for fight or flight. It will take time for them to realise that they can be loved without also being abused.

When children have suffered unpredictable and frightening situations, they feel helpless and anxious when they are not in control. They particularly need consistency. When they feel vulnerable, they can become hostile or withdrawn. The child may cope by becoming very self-reliant or desperate to please or cutting themselves off from their feelings, but all of these responses make it harder to form a meaningful relationship with the child. It is best for foster carers or adoptive parents to consciously resist being drawn into the avoidant, self-reliant and controlling dynamics of the maltreated child. The challenge for the new parents or carers is to remain nurturing even when children give out a message that they do not want care and support or do things to reject or push away the carer.[3]

---

3   See Dozier *et al.* (2002).

CHAPTER 8

Arousal Revisited

I want to think a little bit more about arousal levels (the body's level of physiological readiness for fight or flight) because I have touched on it but haven't really explained it fully. I hope it will be helpful to come back to all of the different aspects of what a child learns from a parent who can hold them in mind, because those things are really important in terms of how that child develops and their mental health. Later, I'll be considering how these issues relate to particular diagnostic labels that might be considered with some children, such as autistic spectrum conditions or attention deficit hyperactivity disorder (ADHD).

From my conversations with adoptive and foster parents, and also with social workers and education staff, it seems that, despite the importance I feel it has in my understanding of looked after and adopted children, arousal level is something that hasn't received enough attention.

As I have mentioned already, basically, what happens is that our life experiences (including the time in the womb) tell our body how ready for fight or flight we need to be. Children who have been exposed to violence produce more cortisol and are more primed for fight or flight. They are sensitised to look for threat signals because the amygdala in the brain is more active and the frontal lobes less so. There is less empathy and ability to reason and more tendency to see situations and other people as a threat, and as a result they tend to have poorer attention and concentration and be more impulsive, resulting in more behaviour problems. The worst combination in terms of neurological development is to have experienced chronic or unpredictable exposure to violence without the affection and nurture that trigger the release of oxytocin, a feel-good neurochemical I mentioned earlier that is related to closeness, empathy and love, which infants release when cuddled or given skin-to-skin contact.

I've tried to draw what happens in your brain and body in terms of physiological arousal (readiness for fight or flight) in Doodle 16, but please don't be put off by it looking a little bit like a graph – no maths is involved!

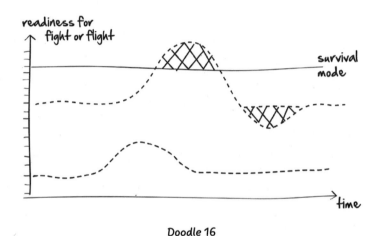

Doodle 16

If you live in calm and safe circumstances, your body might have become used to being at level one on a scale of one to ten in terms of readiness for fight or flight. So, you might be going through your life at one out of ten on a scale of physiological arousal (like the lower dashed line on the chart) and then something stressful might happen: someone might get into an argument with you, someone may drive inconsiderately, you might have to go through an interview experience, and your stress level and your readiness for fight or flight will go up. Your body will release adrenaline and cortisol and it will prime the muscles to get ready to run away. Your blood flow will prioritise a different pattern in your body, where energy is transported to your muscles as opposed to your digestive system. Similarly, different parts of your brain get more or less active according to the amount of adrenaline and cortisol that is around.

On the scale we are using, you might be raised two or three levels by a particular stressor, or even four or five levels by a major source of threat or anxiety. It makes that little hill on the chart. You stay in that state just for a short period of time and normally, as the danger passes or after about half an hour to an hour, your level of arousal comes down and you go back to your normal level. Because you have not reached very high on this scale of arousal, your brain is still quite active and analytical; the frontal parts of your brain that you use for empathy, to self-monitor and to judge cause and effect are still very active, so you can be reasoned with at any point in that process and you can apply logic and learning.

However, if your life experiences have taught you that it is necessary to have a baseline of five or six out of ten readiness for fight or flight because there is a lot of chaos, conflict, trauma and raised voices about, then you might look more like the upper line in the chart. If the same levels of stress that we looked at in the previous example come along (e.g., you get into an argument, someone drives inconsiderately) and you rise the same two or three points on the scale, the results are different. That peak in your arousal level takes you above the threshold at which you go into a kind of survival mode. Something happens within brain activity that means that the amygdala (which is the fight-or-flight sensor in the brain) becomes extremely active. Like a car alarm going off in your brain, it overrides everything else, and the frontal parts of the brain become much less active so your priority becomes just to survive.

When that happens, we are left relying on older parts of the brain, and we go back to very primitive ways of behaving in order to survive. So we fight, we run away, we freeze. We don't think logically, we don't do analysis, we don't do empathy, we don't think through the consequences of our behaviour. Now, that's really helpful as a survival skill, because if you are attacked by a bear, you need to be able to run – and all of your brain activity needs to be focused on picking the best route and scanning for weapons or safe places to hide (not being diverted by wondering about the bear's state of mind or regretting not doing more exercise). If you are attacked by a snake, you may need to fight it off, so your brain will focus on carefully observing the snake's movements and looking for weapons, whilst your body might stay very still to try not to draw its attention. If your child gets stuck under a rock, you don't need logic telling you, 'Oh I probably can't lift that and I don't want to damage my muscles.' You want that surge of adrenaline and blood flow to your muscles that makes you able to lift that rock and move it, no matter what the cost is to your personal health and physical integrity.

So it is a really helpful response in context for the brain to focus on the most critical survival decisions and shut down other functions. But if someone breaks that threshold in a conflict in their family home or school, then there is a peak during which their level of arousal is so high that it is very hard for them to be reasoned with or to apply any empathy or learnt skills at all, because they are in survival mode. At those points, you just have to wait until the adrenaline and cortisol have been burnt off or gone down or do something to soothe the person. If you remember, the soothing system and its chemical messenger oxytocin are the way to trump the messages of cortisol and adrenaline and the activity of the threat system to bring that arousal level down. If you are trying to soothe a child who is in that survival mode, the most helpful calming things you can do are at a non-verbal level, because appealing to reason isn't going to help whilst the appropriate parts of the brain are not active.

It is also worth noting that whilst a person is in a state of high arousal, they tend to interpret neutral signals as being threatening, so even quite benign situations can keep that arousal level high, such as the noise and movement in their classroom at school or any raised tone of voice or sudden noises. They might assume that jokes or partly heard conversations are about them or see facial expressions of concern as being critical.

EMOTIONAL VOLUME

Sometimes it might seem that there is a total mismatch between the level of arousal of the child and the level of arousal in your family, and that the child is constantly drawing you into a state of higher conflict and tension than you would like. If you think about the 'emotional volume' that is happening in a household, it is almost like a car radio. If you have come from a very chaotic household, that car radio has been set very loud and it might not fit in with the volume in the adoptive or foster home. If you imagine driving your car during the course of the day, you might start out at your house by turning the radio on when you turn on the car. Then you might drive on the motorway and turn the volume up a little because of the traffic noise; then there might be a rainstorm or even hail, and you might be stuck in traffic and wanting to hear the news, so you might turn the radio up a bit more. When you park the car for the evening, the radio might still be on the louder setting. When you get up in the morning and go back to the car and turn the engine on, the radio is suddenly too loud because you are not in an environment with enough background noise to merit that level of volume.

I tend to think that, after experiencing trauma or chaotic care, the children who are placed in households where individuals have a secure attachment style after experiencing trauma or chaotic care have a higher set level of volume of emotion or readiness for conflict than is required by that environment. So at some unconscious level they are trying to turn the volume up because that is more familiar, and the parents or carers are trying to turn the volume down. The image of seeking a familiar emotional volume is another way of thinking about this tug of war that is happening at so many levels between the child's attachment pattern and that of their new family.

I mentioned in a previous chapter that the amount of oxytocin a child is used to can also affect the level of physiological arousal they consider to be the normal emotional volume. Most often, this is set so the child is too ready for fight or flight, but it can also be the case that the child's physiology is 'down-regulated' to a lower volume, and they are less aware of risks and less reactive to threats in the environment as a result. I sometimes read in the paperwork about social workers or other professionals noticing that a child doesn't respond to parents shouting or even fighting with each other, as they have become so habituated to it. This is one form of down-regulation. I also previously mentioned in Chapter 5 that down-regulation can be a feature of grooming, sexual exploitation or forms of abuse where the child is made to feel special or rewarded for inappropriate activities.

There can also be cultural elements to the amount of physiological arousal that is considered normal. In a war zone, or when people have undergone dangerous migration journeys or been trafficked, high levels of arousal are an absolutely normal response, but again over time the individual can become habituated to high levels of risk, with their neurochemical responses down-regulated compared to the objective level of threat, depending on their personal physiology and circumstances. The pandemic gave a lot of people a taste of systemic threat that was outside of their control that they had never experienced before. I know that in the early stages I could feel the anxiety in my body. But as with other reactions to experience, different individuals experienced different perceived levels of threat, and different symptoms as a result.

The same rise in fight-or-flight readiness can be true for people who are homeless or living in insecure environments, such as slums, temporary housing or sharing overcrowded accommodation like hostels, hotels or some types of HMOs (Houses in multiple occupancy (where unrelated tenants rent rooms within the same property, and share the use of some areas like kitchens or bathrooms - such as many student houses)). There can also be the threat and trauma of being bullied or victimised, or experiencing racism, religious prejudice, homophobia, transphobia or other forms of discrimination and victimisation. For example, black men and boys are often perceived as 'hypermasculine' and therefore seen as being more threatening and likely to be aggressive by many people in the global north. They are subjected to frequent negative expectations that lead to being disproportionately stopped and searched by police, being treated more negatively and others having lower expectations of them in health, education and employment settings. Understandably, this can lead to frustration and cynicism, which can reinforce negative perceptions. Black males have to work exceptionally hard never to show any negative emotions to avoid being perceived as aggressive. Black women too are easily perceived as angry and aggressive, and learn to avoid showing emotions. This ability to stay calm in stressful situations can be a superpower but it can also come at a price. Our threat perception is a very delicate instrument and the risks of down-regulating it can also lead people into risky situations. Hence the most useful setting is generally to be someone who is able to feel safe and calm, but is sensitive to threats in the environment.

Arousal is quite contagious – when we see someone else rise in their readiness for fight or flight, our own level of physiological arousal intuitively rises to match.[1] I find that fascinating, but it makes a lot of sense in survival terms to be alert to threats perceived by others. What happens is that the more you are around people who are dysregulated (highly emotional and in a state of increased readiness for fight or flight), the more likely you are to dysregulate yourself. So if somebody starts yelling at me, it is very hard physiologically for me to stay calm and not to get ready for fight or flight myself, and if I get ready for fight or flight myself physiologically, it becomes more likely that I perpetuate their dysregulation by shouting back at them. If we try to manage someone who is in fight-or-flight mode, and this makes us a bit anxious or stressed, they might pick up on the slight signs of anxiety we show (like having a faster heart rate, breathing faster, dilated pupils, flushing, etc.) and see them as signs of threat and reasons to stay in fight-or-flight mode themselves, because the body makes the same changes in blood flow whether it is going to use fight or flight, and it can be hard to distinguish between the two unless you know a person really well.

However, just as arousal is quite contagious, so is soothing. This means that if we are calm, then others with us are also calmed by that. When with others who are calm, we are more able to feel relaxed and at ease, particularly when we have soothing sensations or are in skin-to-skin contact with others. You will remember that this is the work of the chemical oxytocin, which is associated with love, sex and nurture.

If we are able to remain calm as adults, we can soothe children and they can feel calmed by it, but when someone dysregulates (e.g.,

---

1   See Nummenmaa *et al.* (2012).

becomes extremely angry or fearful), it instinctively dysregulates us. So it is really important when you are parenting that you don't let the child's behaviour lead you to dysregulate so much that you can't help the child to regulate. This means that when you feel that the child's behaviour is causing you to rise in physiological arousal (signalled by feeling tense, shouting or being physically rougher or more agitated), you really need to use your tag team. If you feel yourself getting angry, your voice getting louder or changing pitch or bodily sensations associated with an increase in physiological arousal (such as sweating, clammy palms, churning stomach, dry mouth, sense of tension or restlessness in the body), this is when you should use your support network and get someone else to come in and support you in both calming down the child and calming down yourself. It is a really good skill to model that you know when you are beginning to dysregulate and can take time out to regulate yourself. Dysregulation doesn't have to lead to conflict.

We also know that children need to learn to co-regulate before they can self-regulate, so if they haven't had that experience of being soothed and cuddled and stroked, then they will find it very hard to bring down their own physiological arousal levels. They will often create or enact some kind of conflict or physical activity until that chemical is burnt out. It is really helpful for those children if we can find a way to help soothe their level of physiological arousal. However, when they are a bit older, it becomes more difficult to pick them up, jiggle them, pat them, stroke them and bring them to your chest as you would a younger child. But ideally you would still do broadly similar things. You would go and sit with them, you would talk in quite an animated loud way to match their level of arousal to acknowledge their distress and then you would gradually start talking more calmly. When it feels safe to do so, you would make some physical contact. Ideally, you would pat them with a rhythm and you would then slow that down and turn it into a stroke, and, wherever possible, you would end up with a physical cuddle that involves skin-to-skin contact and a position where they can hear your heart rate and your breathing rate – much like we talked about when soothing the toddler in an earlier chapter.

Once the child is soothed (and the frontal area of the brain is back online), you can start to explain things to them or appeal to reason and past learning. You might be able to help them connect the story of what has happened into a logical sequence, explaining how they might be feeling. It is good at this point to be aware of the child's shame – the sense that they are a bad child who is unlovable and deserves to be maltreated – and we will return to this in Chapter 14 and consider how we can respond to that in an empathic way. Routine can be helpful and soothing to highly aroused children. To make life predictable and safe, it helps to have the same routine each day (or one for school days and one for other days) and warn children in advance about any expected changes to the routine.

It is also helpful to be aware of the fact that many of their past patterns might be playing out, and their responses might have been learned ways of coping with damaging experiences. Often behaviour communicates what a child can't say in words. I tend to think of the image of an explorer, like Indiana Jones, hacking his way through the jungle towards the temple where he thinks the treasure is hidden. He follows his compass and hacks away a path through the thick foliage with his machete. This takes a lot of effort, because it is cutting a new path, but it is going in exactly the right direction. However, if some threat appears, like someone with a weapon or a predatory animal, he will run where there is already a path. In the same way, it takes traumatised children real effort, energy and dedication to learn new behaviour patterns, and under stress they will behave in old familiar ways, no matter how inappropriate they are or what the consequences will be. The more stress there is, the more cortisol is released and the less the child is able to reason and access learnt behaviours.

However, when a child is in a calm, soothed state, they can begin to use and develop their prefrontal cortex, the most sophisticated and 'human' part of the brain. This area lets us think about thoughts and feelings, the past and the future, and the impact of our behaviour on ourselves and others. It lets us have empathy for other people's experiences and understand that their minds operate in a similar way to our own, although they will have their own goals and preferences, due to having different life experiences. That understanding of the nature of minds is known as 'theory of mind' and is an important building block in social skills. It is the beginning of the reflective capacity that allows us to change how we behave and to challenge our existing patterns (important if we want to form different types of relationships).

Interestingly, recent research suggests that the prefrontal cortex continues to develop throughout childhood and is only completely functional from our early twenties. So this is an area where we continue to develop more and more sophisticated skills for a prolonged period of time and where our experiences and relationships continue to influence our development long beyond the development of the connection patterns in other parts of the brain. However, a rich and stimulating environment and enough calm and safety are required for these pathways to develop. Exposure to ongoing abuse, violence, crime, bullying, racism and sexism (and even media that show these things) can maintain a raised level of fight-or-flight readiness in people who experienced childhood trauma.

I used to think that whether you were in a state of calm or a state of threat was a simple two-sided game of trumps in the brain, according to whether the cortisol or oxytocin was dominant, but I think it makes more sense when you also know about a third system that is at play in the brain that makes me think it might be more like a game of paper, scissors, stone. This third system involves the chemical messenger dopamine and is associated with activity, excitement and the acquisition of status and possessions; in short, anything we find rewarding. It is dopamine that is involved in addiction to any activity and this 'drive' is why we often turn to action when we are distressed, or collect things (or eat or go shopping) in the hope that it will make us happy when we are unable to self-soothe. This is why when attachment doesn't work well and the child doesn't learn to soothe themselves and regulate their physiological arousal, this can increase the risk of dysfunctional patterns in later life, even if this does not show in the form of aggression or anxiety (fight or flight). Again, this will be something we will come back to in later chapters.

CHAPTER 9

The Calm and the Storm

I talked in the last chapter about the pattern of arousal and how this can lead to outbursts or conflict. We also know that these 'blow outs' can be quite reinforcing, by creating the high emotional volume that is familiar to the child and reinforces their perceived sense of threat because they trigger a negative response from those around them. Sometimes when a child or an adult comes out of that patch and they've burnt off a lot of adrenaline and cortisol, there can be a little dip after the big peak on the chart in which they are more able to contact feelings that are vulnerable and empathic and tolerate feeling warm and close to people. This means that the aftermath of a blow out is sometimes found to be very rewarding by the person and those around them, who value the feelings of safety and being close to people after the conflict. That's a tricky situation, because you don't want the aftermath of conflict to be the only time at which you can access the child's more vulnerable feelings, otherwise it reinforces the need to go through this conflict cycle.

As I have mentioned, people who are accustomed to very high levels of fight-or-flight readiness (very high levels of physiological arousal) feel a bit disconcerted in environments that are too quiet and calm because it feels like 'the calm before the storm', and the longer that they are in calm, the more disconcerted they feel, until they create the conflict that allows them to discharge the adrenaline and the cortisol. Obviously, that doesn't happen at a conscious level, but parents often tell me about how it takes smaller and smaller triggers to tip the child into an outburst when they've been having a prolonged period of calm, which is because of the adrenaline and cortisol building up. I sometimes use the metaphor of a training exercise where the facilitator inflates a balloon and asks people to close their eyes whilst they hold the balloon next to each person in turn and scratch the surface to see if it will burst. I would find that a very unpleasant experience, and the worst element would be the lack of control – not knowing whether or when the balloon would burst. Participants in that group would feel very tense, and some might feel a strong urge to reach up and try to pop the balloon to remove the threat and disperse that feeling of tension and anticipation. The threat of violence is much more powerful than the threat posed by a balloon, and the tension caused by anticipating an incident is even more overwhelming.

It is useful to remember that adrenaline is also the messenger involved in excitement, and thus, it is very easy for the physiological arousal that accompanies pleasantly exciting events (such as treats or celebrations, particularly if these are unfamiliar) to switch the child into fight or flight.

The other thing to say about conflict is that we have learnt from domestic violence situations that the victim is often perceived as causing or triggering the violence they experience. This can be a belief held by both the perpetrator and the victim. We hear this shared or displaced attribution of blame in the language of both parties, where they talk about the victim being at fault for causing incidents, and we also see this too often in the media when they talk about domestic violence, and it can even be internalised to some degree by professionals or police dealing with incidents or undertaking assessments.[1] I think we need to be clear that no matter what the provocation, the decision to use physical aggression is never acceptable and is always the responsibility of the perpetrator. However, that doesn't mean that the pattern of how to respond to this threat doesn't become distorted and entrenched in the behaviour

---

1   I've heard some horrible quotes, even from quite famous attachment researchers who say that victims of domestic violence need to take responsibility for 'winding up' the perpetrator, or seem to forget how dangerous it can be to leave such a relationship..

of a person who has previously been a victim of domestic violence, as well as in the perpetrator.

If we think of a heterosexual couple where there is domestic violence from the man towards the woman[2] and the man who has previously perpetrated violence towards her comes home in a state from which she is picking up cues that there might be violence, she will not always act to prevent this. Although it might seem counterintuitive, even if he is giving signals of impending conflict, the woman does not always choose to escape the scene or do everything in her power to avoid the conflict. In many cases, she provokes the conflict (just as the training participant might try to pop the balloon in my earlier metaphor). This may not be a conscious process, but it allows her to have more control, to get it over and done with more quickly and to get to the reward in that dip afterwards where he is saying sorry and telling her he loves her and it will never happen again. This might be the only time he shows authentic vulnerability, and a time when they feel close and have a closer sense of attachment. Obviously, I'm not suggesting that anyone is consciously thinking, 'I'd really like him to hit me now', but there is some kind of skewed learnt logic that subconsciously says, 'If I am in that kind of situation, violence is unavoidable so I might as well get it over and done with and I might as well get to the good bit faster.'

Similarly, a lot of children who have been through traumatic experiences also have that same pattern where if they sense a parent, carer or another person is becoming at all annoyed or threatening (or when it is too calm), they provoke an incident to burn off the conflict as quickly as possible. It makes a great deal of sense as a survival strategy based on their skewed past experience, and they may also have been rewarded by a time of closeness from their parent afterwards. If this is the only way they have experienced

---

2   When explaining this concept, I am using the example of the gender roles that are most commonly reported in domestic violence cases, and I am not intending to imply that domestic violence is exclusively perpetrated by men against women. It is well established that there are perpetrators of all genders, and that domestic violence occurs in same-sex relationships and between many different configurations of family members (e.g., between adult siblings or between parents and their adult children) and similar patterns would apply.

affection or nurture, then they may also provoke an incident when they feel like they need more containment, more affection and more closeness, because that it is their way of getting there. Or if they are very defensive and self-sufficient, they may provoke an incident in order to be able to burn off the fight-or-flight chemistry before they are able to share any vulnerability, and get the physical closeness and comfort they desperately desire. I have heard care-experienced adults talk very movingly about how, as they began to connect with a safe adult for the first time, they needed to test them, and also to be physically close to them for prolonged periods in a way they only knew how to trigger as a restraint, and so they would create the kind of situations that led to restraints rather than being able to make a disclosure or ask for a cuddle any other way.

Case example: Blacking out

I have worked with several young people where their experiences have been vividly described to me as going beyond a rational threshold and losing conscious control of their behaviour. For example, a teenage boy who had been through some really pretty extreme violence at the hands of his parents (including being beaten with a dog chain) had been referred to CAMHS because of episodes in which he in turn had been very violent towards others. When I asked him about those incidents, he would say, 'Something winds me up and then I black out. When I come to, I find out what I have done.' He would talk about 'coming to' having smashed windows, having caused other people injuries or with bruises or blood on his body and not knowing consciously what had been going on, and he found that experience very scary. People around him were sceptical about his apparent 'split personality'. However, I think he was a very extreme example of what happens when the amygdala is so active that the logical, rational, reasonable part of the brain (the frontal area) is switched off for critical periods of time. Sometimes children who have experienced severe abuse early in their lives or where they have no ability to escape or fight back learn to cope with

extreme experiences of violence by blotting them out of awareness, and this dissociation can become an instinctive response
that triggers without any conscious control, as soon as extreme
fear or anger is present. Even having a simple explanation of
what is happening in the brain can normalise what can be a very
frightening experience, and help young people to realise they
are not going mad, but have interrupted memories because of
trauma triggers. The same kind of strategies that we discuss later
in the chapter about 'time holes' can be helpful too.

For someone like this, learning to feel safe and to regulate their own
level of arousal is a really long-term piece of work and may need
specialist therapeutic support. If anger is as extreme as this particular young man described it, then it sometimes really helps to have a
medication that can help bring down the child's heightened physiological arousal so that their baseline is one or two points lower on
the chart and they have a higher capacity before going through that
threshold at which they lose cognitive functioning. This would be
something worth discussing with CAMHS, particularly if there are
frequent and/or severe aggressive episodes or recurrent conflict is
interfering with day-to-day life and normal consequences are not
having an impact.

The effects of trauma, as I have mentioned, are dependent on
dose and timing. We know that the arousal chemicals of adrenaline
and cortisol travel through the placenta, and if the mother is being
exposed to a great deal of domestic violence or conflict or a chaotic
life, then those chemicals will be travelling through the placenta to
warn the baby that life is very dangerous and they need to be primed
for fight or flight. Because heightened arousal levels are so tied in
with our survival instincts, they are remarkably persistent over
time. I've certainly met children of four, five or six who still have a
raised baseline level of physiological arousal because of exposure to
trauma when they were in the womb or as a very young pre-verbal
infant. Some of the most extreme examples of elevated physiological
arousal that I have worked with have been people whose mothers
experienced chaos and trauma during the pregnancy and who were

again exposed to trauma or domestic violence in their very early part of life, which confirmed the necessity of that raised arousal level. Once established, those arousal levels take a long time to change, even in a calmer home. We know that when children witness or experience violence prior to the age of one (and that includes in the womb), it has a profound effect.[3] Children who were exposed to domestic violence during this period still play more aggressively with neutral toys at age six and eight.

⚡ Reflection: Readiness for fight or flight

Have a think about your own life. Have you felt the impact of threat, stress or anxiety at any point? How did it feel in your body? How much control did you have over it? Where are you now on the scale?

How about your child? Did they have reason to feel under threat or stress at any point (including whilst in the womb)? Where are they now on the scale? Does anything cause that to increase or decrease?

It might be worth testing out whether regular exercise or relaxation can influence your child's level of arousal. Exercise would need to be vigorous and sustained enough to burn off the neurochemicals that are having a negative effect, and relaxation would need to be regularly practised and supplemented with relaxing activities. Certain repetitive physical activities can serve both functions, and I have met many families where the trampoline has proved to be an essential piece of kit for this reason. The materials provided by Relax Kids[4] can be useful when it comes to teaching the child to soothe their body and brain, as they include some lovely CDs of relaxation exercises on varied child-friendly themes such as magic, nature and space. It might also be useful to see whether providing feedback to your child by commenting on their state of arousal, and noting times that might potentially be stressful to them (such

---

3   See Carpenter and Stacks (2009) and O'Connor *et al.* (2002).
4   www.relaxkids.com

as long periods of calm), can help them to pre-empt dysregulating. Therapy techniques such as Theraplay, a method of using playful activities to compensate for missed nurture experiences and improve the attachment relationship, can also build on this. I've also seen music and rhythm used effectively to help young people learn to self-soothe and regulate their emotions.

CHAPTER 10

Diagnoses

I have discussed in earlier chapters how the attuned care of a secure caregiver teaches a child to self-regulate, have a positive self-image and learn the building blocks of empathy and social skills. Where these are absent, it can end up looking like certain developmental disorders (see Doodle 17). As I have detailed, exposure to chronic trauma during development leads a child to have a heightened readiness for fight or flight and to emotionally dysregulate more easily. As I explained in the previous two chapters, we know that the increased presence of cortisol and adrenaline has a profound effect on the body and brain. We know that raised levels of arousal are associated with changes in blood flow in the body, with increased blood supply to the muscles and less to the organs and digestive system. There are also changes to which sections of the brain are more active, with more activity in the primitive brain and less in the sophisticated prefrontal areas.

These changes in blood flow and brain activity often show in the child's behaviour as difficulties with concentrating, higher levels of motor activity, being more impulsive, having less ability to see the consequences of actions, difficulty reading social cues and an increased tendency towards aggression. All of those look like what is known as ADHD (attention deficit hyperactivity disorder, which may be subdivided into 'inattentive' and 'hyperactive' subtypes, and was sometimes called the more old-fashioned name of 'hyperkinetic disorder' in the UK). My own research shows that about half of children undergoing family court cases and half of children in Care who require a psychological assessment show clinically significant levels of ADHD-like symptoms, compared with only 2 per cent of children in the general population. Although trauma-based hyperarousal might look superficially like ADHD, biochemically it is hypothesised to be from a very different cause.[1] ADHD is hypothesised to be a lack of activity in the frontal areas of the brain for neurochemical reasons, whilst traumatic hyperarousal is caused by overactivity in the amygdala leading to shut-down of the frontal areas. ADHD is therefore often treated with stimulant medications that increase that frontal activity, whereas chronic exposure to trauma might need a different form of treatment, as there is already a heightened level of arousal in the brain.[2]

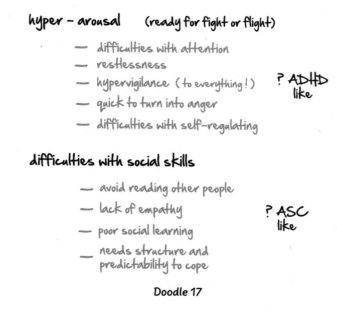

Doodle 17

However, we know that children who have been maltreated have a much higher risk of neurodevelopmental disorders, and that children with neurodevelopmental disorders have a higher risk

---

1 However, the research to date has not identified a simple difference in brain chemistry or anatomy or a single genetic carrier for ADHD, suggesting that it might be a combination of different factors.
2 See Teicher *et al.* (2003).

of maltreatment.[3] So many children may have both the impact of early trauma and attachment difficulties and a diagnosable neurodevelopmental condition. They might also have a higher risk of exposure to drugs or alcohol in the womb, leading to foetal drug or alcohol spectrum disorders. Other diagnostic labels that might overlap with the presenting features of exposure to trauma and poor experiences of attachment include those on the autistic spectrum. This is a cluster of conditions where the brain is not set up to process information in the same way as the majority of people. The typical results of these differences are difficulties with social understanding, difficulties with flexibility of thinking and difficulties with the social aspects of communication. This means that people with autism might struggle to make friends, to behave in a socially appropriate way and to cope with unpredictable variations to their routine and might not be able to adapt their communication to the audience (typically, monologuing on topics they are particularly interested in, without reference to the response of the person they are talking to). They often have difficulties recognising emotions and a poor understanding of the thoughts and feelings of others.

Autistic behaviours are often associated with the tendency to need a lot of order and structure (e.g., lining up toys or being very precise about time, or becoming anxious or unable to cope when plans change) and/or differences in response to sensory information (e.g., reduced reaction to pain, enjoyment of patterns and lights, highly sensitive hearing). People with autism spectrum conditions also have increased rates of other neurodevelopmental and brain-related conditions including learning difficulties and disabilities, tics, fits, attention difficulties, language problems, dyspraxia (lack of motor coordination, often including clumsiness) and other developmental difficulties. People with autism also have a tendency to become preoccupied with narrow interests, to collect factual data and to be confused by subtle expressions of emotion. They often struggle to adapt to different circumstances or to understand what is expected of them unless it is explained in a very specific and concrete way.

---

3   See Dinkler *et al.* (2017).

Autism is a spectrum of different presentations, which range from quite a subtle pattern to one that is profoundly disabling. The extent to which autism impairs functioning is also affected by the level of ability the person has (generally, it is much more disabling when combined with learning disability), the nature of any other difficulties they have (e.g., ADHD, epilepsy, dyspraxia, language disorder, Tourette's syndrome) and the amount of support and structure that is available to them. They may also have various strengths (e.g., in visual or technical skills, or in seeing things differently). Sometimes the milder presentations or those where the person is highly intelligent are missed or only recognised in adulthood. People with these patterns of difference where there is not an intellectual or language delay may be given the diagnostic label of Asperger syndrome or high functioning autism, or they might be given a label of autistic spectrum disorder (ASD) or autism spectrum condition (ASC), as the diagnostic labels vary between individuals and over time. I will use the acronym ASC to refer to presentations on this spectrum to remind us that the differences indicated by this label can vary enormously from person to person, although most people on the spectrum choose to refer to themselves as autistic.

If a person has ASC, the extent of their difficulties may appear different at different times in their life. The number of problems they experience and the amount to which their behaviour is atypical or would be viewed as noticeably odd to others with neurotypical[4] social skills varies according to their development or the amount of stress they are experiencing. Some people can appear to be profoundly autistic in their early childhood, but their presentation can become more and more subtle as they develop and learn compensatory skills, such that they can function very well as an adult (see Temple Grandin's autobiographical works,[5] for example). Others can appear more able but regress or show more unusual behaviour

---

4   Neurotypical is a label people with ASC give to those of us who don't have ASC, who appear strangely preoccupied with socialising and the thoughts and feelings of others.

5   See Grandin (2006), Grandin (2008) and Grandin and Scariano (2005).

when under stress or where there is significant change or uncertainty (e.g., when changing school or when on holiday).

People with ASC seem to see the world in a more logical and mechanised way, struggle to understand the nature of people who have thoughts and feelings that are not visible, and might act in ways that are not always rational and predictable. There has been a lot of research exploring the nature of this difference (which appears to be at least partly a genetic trait) and trying to localise differences in the brain, though the exact mechanism is still a mystery. However, it is clear that people with autism have a less intuitive sense of how other people think and feel. We call this 'theory of mind': having a working model of the nature of subjective experience. You might remember that we mentioned this when we covered how attachment patterns transmit from one generation to the next.

Research indicates that to gain an effective theory of mind you need both inbuilt biological capacity in the brain (which, it is hypothesised, people with ASC lack) and the early experiences of being held in mind by another, normally your parent or carer. This process of someone constantly considering what you think or feel and reflecting your emotions back to you allows you to learn to recognise and name your emotions, learn to regulate them, experience empathy and learn to use the frontal parts of your brain to be aware of your own thoughts and feelings and those of others. This may be absent, or much less consistent or effective, for people with early abuse and neglect.

You will see from the above descriptions that there can be considerable overlap between the presentations of people with ASC and those who have experienced poor early care and abuse. For example, there are many academic papers published about the 'quasi-autistic' presentations of children removed from the highly deprived orphanages of eastern Europe.[6] When the adopted Romanian orphans were four years old, many showed a pattern of difficulties indistinguishable from autism. By six years old, some were showing more flexibility in communication and a more social approach but

---

6   See Rutter *et al.* (2007).

sometimes indiscriminate friendliness. After their adoption, many had developed circumscribed and repetitive interests. At 11 years old, the researchers followed up all the adoptees with social communication problems and did a thorough assessment and diagnosis. One in nine of the adoptees showed the quasi-autistic pattern, but they were more likely to lose some of these features as they grew older than children in the general population with ASC.

As these very extreme examples of deprivation show, it seems that severe neglect or chronic poor care can lead children to present in a very similar way to autism. The nature of the brain, which remains highly plastic for much of early childhood, means that it is often difficult to distinguish the source of any impairment. However, there are some distinguishing features that I've been exploring in my research.[7] Possibly the most obvious differentiating factor between ASC children and those who have experienced abuse and neglect is how the children relate to adults. Children with ASC tend to relate to adults just like any other object in their environment and not pay them too much attention, or see them as a tool to get things they want and ignore them at other times, whilst many children who have experienced abuse and poor early care are very vigilant towards adults, even if they don't respond to them in the same ways as children who have experienced good enough care. Children with ASC also tend to be blithely oblivious to teasing or social rejection from their peers, whilst those who have experienced abuse or neglect are very sensitive to signs of rejection and may even interpret neutral cues negatively (e.g., interpreting a concentrating facial expression as one that is cross with them). There is increasing interest in how you differentiate ASC from the impact of abuse and neglect, and in the incidence of ASC amongst children in Care and adopted children. However,

---

7   It seems that people with ASD and those who have experienced abuse and neglect both have poor theory of mind and struggle to understand other people's thoughts and feelings. However, children with ASD seem to give more incorrect explanations as to why other people use non-literal language than those with poor early experiences, who are more likely to express confusion or give a physical explanation instead.

there is still a need for more research about the outcomes for the two different groups.

It is also worth acknowledging that a lot of children who are in the Care system might also have organic difficulties, as well as having experienced social adversity. This can include the impact of foetal exposure to drugs or alcohol. Children in the looked after and adopted system have higher proportions of certain kinds of conditions than those in the general population. This would include a range of developmental disorders like ASC, ADHD, learning disability and mental health conditions. The reason for this is twofold. First, parents with these kinds of traits are more likely to have difficulties with providing good enough care for their child and therefore are more at risk of having their child removed into Care. Second, children with these kinds of traits are more challenging to parent effectively and are likely to show more profound impairments more obviously when given deficient care.[8] It may be that a parent can just about cope with meeting the needs of a developmentally typical child but struggles to meet the needs of a child with a developmental disorder. Of course, it may also be that profound neglect and exposure to poor care can actually cause changes to the brain as well as missed or dysfunctional learning experiences that lead the child to appear developmentally disturbed.

This is a complicated subject for professionals to consider because there is a tendency to assume that if you see certain symptoms, they are diagnostic of a biological condition, or if a child has been through abuse or neglect, that becomes an explanatory factor for everything they are presenting. Probably the wisest path is somewhere in between the two: to acknowledge that there are often combinations of organic and acquired difficulties. Such combinations are often bigger than the sum of their parts, in the sense that the combination of a disorder, like ASC, ADHD or learning disability, and adverse experiences, like having been abused or neglected, can

---

8   Looked after children are more likely to have developmental disorders or mental health problems. See Ford *et al.* (2007) and Howard, Kumar and Thornicroft (2001).

create incredibly challenging presentations, much more so than one of these conditions alone.

Case example: I don't understand the risk

I was asked to assess a 15-year-old young girl called Lindsey on the children's ward after an episode of deliberate self-harm. She had taken an overdose of cough medicine, and it was the 19th time she had been known to A&E since moving into the area two years before. Each time, she had called an ambulance for similar reasons, such as having drunk shampoo, eaten unidentified berries or taken tablets. When I went to assess her, I was able to read her health and social care notes, and neither contained any record of any underlying condition. However, both made reference to how she had experienced abuse and neglect, and then multiple changes of placement, and was 'a very troubled young woman'. I felt that she had difficulty understanding which substances she was consuming genuinely posed a risk to her health. She was unable to understand that taking eight co-codamol tablets might be very dangerous to her health or even fatal, whilst 20 vitamins or cough sweets might pose less risk.

When I completed a cognitive assessment and explored her level of social understanding and theory of mind, I found that Lindsey had a moderate learning disability (her IQ was in the bottom one child per thousand, meaning that her understanding would have been more typical of a child of under four years of age). She also had very poor theory of mind, obsessions about the route that her foster carers drove to different locations (including the numbers on the lampposts they passed and whether the cat was sat on the right wall) and a number of narrow, rigid interests suggesting autistic traits. The underlying developmental disorder, despite it being really quite serious, had been overlooked because of what was known about her history.

We were able to work with her carers and the local ambulance crews and A&E staff to ensure that she had a very boring experience of being taken to hospital and waiting for blood tests and was sent home to await the test results without being admitted to the children's ward unless medical treatment was necessary. We also added numerous nurturing activities that would be offered when she had not self-harmed for a few days, such as doing face packs, hair styling, nail polish or hand massage with her carer. Most importantly, the level of autonomy that was expected of Lindsey was reduced to a developmentally appropriate level, and greater support was offered in education, which reduced her levels of stress. Over the following month, the incidents of self-harm reduced, and she had only one ambulance call-out in the following year.

If you suspect that your child also has an organic disorder, professionals may need to help you map your child's development over time to differentiate the two, and it may be that combinations of strategies will need to be tested out, including those that are relevant to particular conditions as well as those that are relevant to traumatised and neglected children. However, as a general rule of thumb, the interventions that are helpful for neurodivergent children such as those on the autistic spectrum or with ADHD are helpful and not harmful for children who have attachment difficulty and whose symptoms are there because of exposure to trauma or neglect. Similarly, the strategies that are helpful to children who are traumatised or neglected are helpful rather than harmful to children who have neurodevelopmental disorders.

One of the strategies that is useful for both groups of children is to always remember that they have a limited understanding of the social world and of how other people think or feel. Whenever you are discussing an incident with them, always include the social information they may not know. For example, they might be hit by another child and think they are being bullied for no reason, because they do not always understand their part in the build-up to what the other child did. They may not be able to differentiate what is accidental and what is deliberate or to understand other people's motivations. For example, you may need to explain that the other child did not like it when they pushed them off the trampoline, that other children like to share and that the trampoline belongs to all the children. It was not right for that child to hit them, but it was also not right to push them off the trampoline. Similarly, it is not enough to tell them not to grab items from others, without explaining that other children don't like it when things they are playing with get taken, that each person should have a turn with an item and that other children will not like to play with them if they grab items when it is not their turn.

CHAPTER 11

Understanding Thoughts, Feelings and Behaviours

Clinical psychologists don't work to a medical model in which symptoms are seen to represent underlying disease that can be diagnosed and treated with medication. We like to look at a wide range of biological, social and psychological factors that combine to make a particular presentation, often grouping these into predisposing factors, underlying beliefs, triggers and maintaining cycles, and look at how these lead to challenging behaviour, emotional distress or difficulties in relating to others. We call this process 'formulation', and it is used to try to understand what has led up to a behaviour, what influences it and what interventions might help it to change.

Don't worry if you have not heard the word 'formulation' before. The concept of formulation is not frequently used outside of applied psychology, but I see it as absolutely key in deciding how to intervene with any child, adult or family. Along with prompting us to conduct a holistic multi-dimensional assessment (one that looks at the individual in a broad way, considering what is going on in their life and how they are feeling), formulation allows us to individualise our understanding of a person we are working with, and thus create an individualised intervention, which may draw on many models. This ability to individualise our intervention for each person, rather than use one intervention in a one-size-fits-all way, is something I regard as being key to successful interventions and one of the best things about being a clinical psychologist. You can see an outline formulation in Doodle 18.

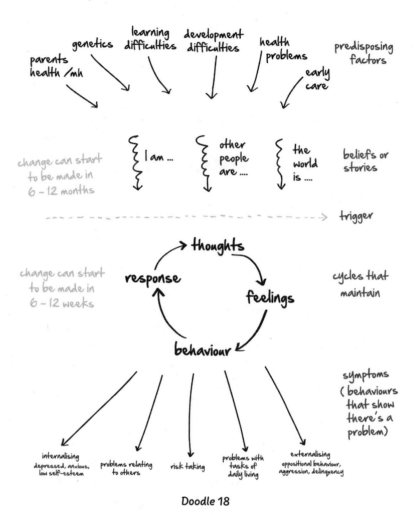

Doodle 18

Factors like a child's genes, their level of ability, their temperament and any physical disability or learning difficulties are organic examples of predisposing factors. However, early experience will also normally go under this heading because it is something that we cannot change which has a lasting effect on the child. This might include exposure to violence, a lack of early nurture, exposure to excessive criticism and emotional harm, sexual abuse, poor early diet and/or stimulation, exposure to parental mental health problems or drug/alcohol use or violence (including whilst in the womb).

These early experiences will lead the child to form a set of core beliefs about how the world is, what other people are like and what they are like as a person. If they have had healthy nurturing experiences and caregivers who have enjoyed being with them and positively reflected what they are experiencing, then the child will build a sense of themselves as being alright or a good person, other people as being mostly kind and well intentioned and the world as an interesting and mostly safe place. If their experiences are of neglect, chaotic living circumstances, violence, unpredictable or harmful caregivers, criticism, rejection and a lack of positive engagement, then the beliefs they form about themselves, the world and others will be very different. They might believe that they are bad or broken or worthless, that other people are dangerous, deceptive or unreliable and that the world is a scary place full of danger.

As I mentioned earlier, these core beliefs have a profound effect on the rest of that person's life, because they determine their self-image, how much they trust others and how ready for fight or flight they must remain. These core beliefs can also form the rules by which the child believes the world works. For example: 'I am completely bad, and when people recognise that they reject me', 'Other people only like me when I meet their needs', 'It is better not to risk trusting others' or 'Other people inevitably let you down.' Once these beliefs are in place, any trigger event or stressor can make them show.

Around the core beliefs is a layer of cycles that maintain the current situation. In their simplest form, these are cycles of thoughts, feelings and behaviours within a single individual. For example, if a person is afraid of spiders, then they might see one and think, 'Oh no, it's a spider! I can't cope, I must run away and get someone else to deal with it.' They might feel really anxious, and their behaviour might include leaving the room or calling for help so that someone else deals with the spider. Of course, that does not allow the person to learn anything new about spiders or their ability to cope with them, and so the next time they see a spider, the pattern repeats. As a therapist, the easiest intervention point is in challenging the thoughts about the spider (because, after all, spiders in the UK can't actually do anything bad to people and don't really merit the level of fear and disgust they provoke) and in helping the person to manage their anxiety (e.g., by taking deep breaths) and to change their behaviour (stay in the room, have a look at the spider, maybe even catch it with a pint glass and a piece of card and tip it outside the window). Each of these things allows the person to feel more effective and create a less negative cycle.

The other thing that happens with maintenance cycles is that they draw in other people. In the example above, there is someone who will come in and deal with the spider so that the anxious person doesn't have to. And often, despite their best intentions, as in this example, other people's actions allow or reinforce the unwanted behaviour – here the helper unwittingly reinforces the fear of the spider, and the inability of the individual to deal with it themselves. The behaviours of the individual will also affect the thoughts and feelings of the other person. For example, a child who is reluctant to accept affection might lead the caregiver to have thoughts about the child not liking them, or perhaps it touches a particularly sore spot of thoughts about being a failure as a parent. These thoughts and feelings might affect how that caregiver is able to behave towards the child. And, of course, there may be more than one other person, so the thoughts, feelings and behaviours of a partner, your parents, neighbours or teachers might also come into play. This means that when I make a formulation about what is going on for a particular child, I am particularly interested in how their behaviour impacts on other people in their network and how the behaviour of other people in the network impacts on the child.

Case example: I never get presents

I worked with an adoptive family who were struggling with having very different expectations of their daughter, Elsie, when compared with those of her school. The family felt that Elsie (who was about eight years old) was bright but preferred to act immaturely and put in little effort. So they were trying to encourage her to act more maturely and be responsible for her own choices. They felt that the school, and in particular the classroom support assistant, was quite overindulgent with Elsie. She would often come home with small gifts, like cuddly toys or dressing up-clothes, or mention having biscuits. Eventually the parents were informed that the school had made a child-protection referral. Elsie had told them that her father had hit her and she was scared of him. The parents were very anxious about the child-protection process and denied that the reported events had taken place. Social workers who investigated found no evidence to substantiate the allegation.

When I worked with the family and spoke to the school, it became clear that Elsie had an insecure ambivalent attachment style and had found it effective within her family of origin to make others feel sympathy towards her. When her birth mother felt guilty for hitting her, Elsie would be given sweets and gifts, and when she looked sad and vulnerable, visitors would give her treats or cuddles. Within the school, she had found that telling tales of how deprived she was at home, and how she never got presents, allowed her to get out of activities she did not like, gain second helpings of pudding and get treats and small gifts from her classroom support assistant (who was a doting grandmother to her own family). However, it also transpired that the adoptive father was occasionally using smacking[1] as a consequence for challenging behaviour, and this had made her fearful because it reminded her of the assaults she had experienced in the birth family. We were able to work on meeting Elsie's need for nurture but also to encourage autonomy, in collaboration with the school. We also worked on acknowledging Elsie's past experiences and using effective parenting strategies to build more positive relationships within the family.

---

1 Although I do not believe that smacking is a helpful or effective method of shaping children's behaviour, and the evidence shows that it is harmful for children's psychological development, the example given was considered to be within the law and thus was something we worked on changing rather than viewed as a child-protection issue.

In terms of intervention, we know that certain models of therapy can make significant changes to the way people think, feel and behave within 6–12 weeks. Probably the most widely known of these is Cognitive Behaviour Therapy (often shortened to CBT), which is a way of exploring these maintenance cycles, challenging negative thinking and undertaking small experiments to test out the objective truth of certain ideas that the individual believes as incontrovertible truth.

It is much harder to access and change a person's underlying core beliefs. Therapy might help to tackle individual symptoms or maintenance cycles, but other symptoms or cycles might continue to emerge to replace them until a very entrenched belief starts to shift. This means that even with skilled therapy, we expect change to only start to be visible in 6–12 months of work. However, the evidence is good that change is possible, and an increasing number of specialist therapies have been developed and researched that have been shown to be effective in changing core beliefs and entrenched patterns of relating to others. These include what are known as the 'third-wave' cognitive therapies, such as Schema Therapy, Compassionate Mind work, Dialectical Behaviour Therapy, and Cognitive Analytic Therapy. These are particularly helpful with articulate adolescents and adults who are processing historic experiences of childhood trauma.

When working with parents and children specifically looking at attachment issues, models such as Dyadic Developmental Psychotherapy (which works with parents, and then the parent and child together in a pair or 'dyad'), Theraplay (which uses playful interactions between parent and child), Life Stage Integration[2] and the Attachment and Bio-behavioural Catch-up Intervention[3] are starting to show promise. Psycho-educational groups for foster and adoptive parents, such as my group, Managing Behaviour with Attachment in Mind, have also shown high levels of efficacy in helping caregivers feel more skilled to meet the needs of children

___

2   See Siegel (2006).
3   See Dozier, Lindhiem and Ackerman (2005).

with challenging presentations learnt from poor early care, trauma, abuse and neglect.[4]

As I said in Chapter 6, about how attachment difficulties pass from one generation to another, there are many opportunities to make changes in a person's attachment style. This can happen at any point across the entire lifespan, and any significant positive relationship can be the catalyst to start that process. However, a skilled psychological therapist can be particularly helpful at understanding the full map of all the issues and how they play out between all the individuals involved. A comprehensive assessment and formulation can help everyone to understand what is going on and to work out what specific areas of change might be most helpful to focus on to make progress. That might include working with parents or carers on their beliefs or reactions to the child, as well as working with the child, or working with members of the family together.

Overall, there is every reason to feel optimistic that change is possible but also to be realistic about the amount of time and effort required.

4   See Holmes and Silver (2010).

CHAPTER 12

Parenting with PACE

When I run my groups for adoptive and foster carers, we often talk about how you begin to make up for some of those missed experiences we highlighted in the brick-wall exercise. Dr Dan Hughes, an American clinical psychologist, has been incredibly important in studying how we repair damaged attachment patterns. He is one of the people who has really taught us about the core skills that help to re-parent traumatised children. I went out to America in 2005 to train with him, and it had a huge impact on my way of being as a therapist.

I had always been taught to keep a kind of neutrality with the children, adults and families that I worked with, without showing too much emotion or getting too personally involved. I was persuaded by the historically accepted notion that the best method of therapy was to form a relationship that gradually circled the problem, slowly getting a little closer until the individual brought up the issue or made a disclosure, or the relationship was strong enough to talk about the real business that brought us together. Unfortunately, with this technique, a lot of people disengage from therapy or are moved on before you get to the most important bit. Similarly, if foster or residential carers circle but never speak about the main issues until they know a child really well, the child may end up moving placement before the topic is ever discussed properly.

Dan Hughes turned all this on its head for me. He said that provided you create certain qualities in the relationship right from the start, to allow the child to feel safe and foster moments of genuine connection and shared feelings, you can touch on the main topic of concern very early in the relationship. You can mention it head on and then show that the relationship is safe by using ideas of 'break and repair'. So before I explain Dan Hughes' main techniques for re-parenting a child whose early care has been damaging, I will explain the idea of break and repair.

To a young child, any form of criticism or boundary can feel like an interruption to the normal flow of the relationship. A caregiver's comment that a behaviour is unacceptable can feel to the child as if they are unacceptable, because the child hasn't yet formed a strong sense of self that can be separated from what they are doing or how they feel in the moment. As a result, any negative feedback can feel like a rejection, a break in the relationship, that feels incredibly vulnerable until it is repaired and the child is clear that they are still loved and accepted.

As I mentioned in Chapter 5, infants learn to regulate their level of readiness for fight or flight with the help of their parents. At first they need an adult to co-regulate their arousal and recognise what caused those feelings, but this is gradually internalised. By the time children are a bit older, we expect them to be able to modulate their own level of physiological arousal because we tell them to have some time out to calm down, sit on the naughty step or go to their room until they are calmer. With older children, we leave that regulation to them more and more.

However, with a child who has not experienced consistent and attuned early care, you need to actively repair the relationship each time you break it, in order to build trust that it is the behaviour that is unacceptable to you and that, despite the criticism, the child is still loved. For the child who has experienced rejection, neglect or abuse, any criticism feels like a break in the relationship and you then have to make good that relationship so that the child learns to change the behaviour whilst retaining a sense of themselves as loveable and their relationship with the caregiver as safe. Dan Hughes would add to the arousal regulation the idea that if we tell a child off for what they are doing, we have to help them to regulate and we have to tell them that the relationship is okay.

From my observations of parents, I think many people do this intuitively with little children. If a toddler touches something potentially dangerous we say, 'No no, don't put your fingers in the socket! Come on, let's play over here', which is a break and a repair in very quick succession. What's interesting is that by the time a child is a teenager, we often say to them, 'Go to your room and think about what you have done', and we don't actively repair that relationship. We don't actively come back and reprocess that and say, 'You know what, you're a good kid, and you're alright with me. It was just that thing you did that was annoying.' Dan Hughes teaches us that whenever we use a criticism, or whenever the child is in a state of distress, we have to repair that relationship much more quickly and actively if the child has had experiences of trauma or abuse in their background.

Case example: A very naughty girl!

When I think back to my childhood, there was a time when I was about nine years old where I was very difficult for a babysitter. I refused to go to bed when she said it was bedtime and stayed downstairs no matter what consequences she promised or threatened. When she heard my parents returning from their night out, she offered me one last chance to go to bed quickly, offering to tell my parents I had been good and gone to bed at the normal time if I did so. I still refused, and my parents returned to find me downstairs. I remember thinking they would be very cross with me for being so disobedient, so when my dad said 'Go to bed now, we'll deal with you tomorrow', I thought there would be some kind of punishment when I woke up. However, when I woke up, life went on as normal. Amazingly, they appeared to have forgotten! So I anxiously waited for them to remember and give me my overdue punishment. Hours, days, weeks, months passed. Eventually I asked them about it, fearing I was going to get some long-awaited consequence. My dad said, 'Oh, I was probably trying to show the babysitter I was standing up for her rules, but I just wanted you to go to bed. From my point of view, you went to bed the first time I had asked. I don't think I ever intended there to be any more consequence than that.'

I look back on this incident and see that even for a securely attached child who had never experienced abuse or neglect, that little break in the relationship needed to be repaired for me to feel okay about myself and my place in the family. Through that, I can understand how essential it is to provide a repair that happens as soon as, and is as obvious as, possible for children who have experienced trauma, rejection and maltreatment. It's only normal to have times in which we get angry or we say something critical towards our children, but the important thing is that we give the message that despite this (and even during this), we still love the child as a whole. Dan Hughes recommends 'sixty-second scolding' in which you express your frustration for no longer than a minute before repairing the relationship. It sounds like that would be impossible, but a minute is a really long time to try and maintain an angry monologue in practice!

CORE QUALITIES OF A THERAPEUTIC PARENT

As I have said before, the task of re-parenting a child who has been damaged by their past experiences is much more difficult than the task of parenting an untraumatised birth child. I believe that to be most successful, you need to create certain therapeutic qualities in how you parent that child. Dan Hughes talks about parenting with PACE.[1] These acronyms allow him to talk about the key qualities of an attachment relationship in which you wish to re-parent a child whose prior care has not been good enough. These qualities, as you can see in Doodle 19, are being Playful, Accepting, Curious and Empathic, with an overarching theme of showing the child that they are loved. It is useful to think about what each of those things means in some depth.

We know that some of the best experiences to have in childhood are where people are *Playful*, immersed in a shared experience and enjoying each other's company. There are moments of playfulness where you end up giggling until your belly hurts and those when the

1   See Hughes (2007).

focus is nothing but having some shared fun. Those shared experiences of joy are great ways for parents to experience and share the positive aspects of interacting with their child. So it is really important to keep the tone playful whenever possible. To use your relationship as an agent of change, you don't want to get stuck in a pattern of criticising, teaching or being aloof and leaving the child to themselves. You really want to get in there and be playing with the child and reflecting back to them how much you enjoy being with them. This doesn't only mean doing playful activities with the child, such as using toys or going to the park, but also includes how you interact with them verbally. When you are playful, you pay attention to what they are experiencing, you interact in ways intended to amuse them and you enjoy being with them. One example of a very simple game is the 'One, two, three, tickle' game that many parents play with a baby. They establish a rhythm of the counting and movement occurring and then slightly slow it down or speed it up to confound the infant's expectations, and everybody involved enjoys it and shares smiles, giggles and eye contact.

Playful

Loving

Accepting

Curious

Empathic

Doodle 19

A game can be any form of playful interaction. Playfulness is inherently enjoyable and engaging, and if you can find a playful way to present a task, the child is more likely to comply and produce the desired behaviour. Perhaps the tidying up that the child does not want to do can be offered as various games and challenges that they might enjoy – like throwing items into a basket, or taking turns folding the same garment. Playfulness can make even the most mundane of daily activities into a positive attachment experience. For example, a friend of mine used to wrap her children so they were covered in a large towel after a bath and then say 'Is this parcel for me? I wonder what is in it? It feels like it might be something lovely like a teddy bear. Oh, it's something soft and giggly... I wonder what it can be?' whilst feeling and tickling the 'parcel'. Or you can play 'delicious or disgusting' whilst naming items to eat, from earthworms to pizza, or you can pass the time on a car journey by playing 'I Spy'. You may be talented or uninhibited enough to sing songs together, or fit enough to run around, jump and climb together. Maybe you can tell stories that include items the child chooses, or decide what sound and movement each type of food has when spoon-feeding. When my children were five to seven years old, I made a game called 'Food Explorers' to encourage them to try unfamiliar foods, where we'd draw a treasure map and a boat or character could get one step nearer the treasure for each mouthful eaten – perhaps the beetroot would get the boat through the treacherous rocks, or the beans would let the pirate climb the mountain trail. It completely flipped the script on the frustration I felt when they refused things I had taken time to prepare, to them being brave adventurers who enjoyed eating a really wide range of foods. Playfulness is about creating joyful shared experience.

To be *Accepting* is about acknowledging that the child's memories, beliefs and feelings are valid, and that (even if you want to help change their behaviour) the child is how they are right now and that you accept the whole of them. You accept the fact that there is a whole lot of traumatic stuff that has gone before, which makes them behave in a number of challenging and different ways, but you consider that the whole child they are right now, complete with all that baggage, is still acceptable and worth loving. That is a really powerful message to convey to a child who may not perceive themselves as loveable or worthy. Given that a lot of children who have experienced trauma, abuse or neglect feel that they are inherently bad people, and the cause of their maltreatment, feeling loved unconditionally might be a new experience. To acknowledge that the child is distressed and carries with them a lot of baggage but to still consider them acceptable as a whole may be something they have never experienced, and is a remarkably powerful message. Several children I have worked with have asked their parents questions like 'If I broke your favourite vase, would you still love me? If I hurt you, would you still love me? If I killed someone, would you still love me?' to test how far this acceptance goes. There are a few lovely children's books that carry this message in rhyming verse, which shows how universal and significant the experience of being accepted is.

Accepting your child exactly as they are also helps them to see that they are loveable and worthy of a good life even when the world has been unkind to them or they have been told that they are less than in some way. I have mentioned that there are various experiences that can also shape a child's sense of themselves, others and the world. As well as abuse and neglect, these could include exposure to conflict or war, famine, natural disasters, migration, living in temporary camps or fighting for legal rights. Refugees often experience a wide range of traumatic events, including violence, persecution, loss of family members, trafficking and exploitation. These experiences can lead to feelings of fear, anxiety and hope-lessness. Furthermore, refugees are often separated from their support systems, cultural norms and sense of identity, which can lead to feelings of isolation and dislocation. The experience of being a refugee is a unique type of trauma that can have lasting effects on an individual's mental health.

But even if a child grew up in a safe home in a safe country, many people experience recurrent emotional injuries from bullying, racism, sexism, homophobia, ableism or other forms of prejudice. These can become internalised as truths about the world, and make children feel negative or conflicted about their identity. Even feeling okay about your body and appearance is a challenge for many people, and finding body-positive role models and reaching acceptance of ourselves that isn't conditional on weight loss, lighter skin or conforming to popular beauty standards can be life-changing.

People of African and Caribbean heritage, Jews and Gypsy, Roma and Irish Travellers may also be impacted by historical trauma – the emotional and psychological wounds that result from the traumatic experiences that their ancestors have endured. These experiences can include slavery, colonialism, segregation and the Holocaust. Historical trauma can be passed down from generation to generation and can have a lasting impact on mental health and well-being. People of colour also experience ongoing trauma due to the disproportionate levels of violence they face. People of colour are more likely to experience violence in their communities and are more likely to have negative experiences of police and the criminal justice system. Structural, institutional and individual acts of racism can mean that people of colour experience discrimination in various aspects of their lives, such as education, employment, housing and healthcare. This can cause significant stress, anxiety and trauma, which can lead to various mental health issues. If you are caring for a child with a different ethnicity, or with a different experience of their race or identity, recognising and empathising with this is an essential part of understanding their experience. Even very young children may have internalised negative ideas about their value, attractiveness or future prospects, due to racism. Positive feedback and role models are particularly important in this situation.

There are also forms of cultural oppression that change our whole sense of self, such as messages from family or religious/cultural groups that lead to people not feeling able to show their authentic sexuality or gender identity. Individuals who experience intersectional adversity, or the experience of being marginalised across multiple social categories (such as race, gender, sexual orientation, socioeconomic status and disability), are particularly vulnerable and may be at increased risk for a range of mental health problems. Intersectional adversity can lead to a sense of social exclusion, discrimination and stigmatisation, which can contribute to feelings of hopelessness, helplessness and lack of control.

When sensitised by any of these experiences, messages about being unworthy in some way (or experiences of others and the world being unsafe), can be reinforced by the ongoing forms of oppression that many people in minority groups experience in their day-to-day life and see portrayed repeatedly in the media. Comments that are intended as jokey or seen as part of the normal banter in certain contexts or topical issues of political debate can feel personal and even threatening.

Accepting the child in their entirety, even if their understanding of themselves or identity changes over time, is an essential component of being a supportive caregiver. Feeling accepted for who we are and finding loving relationships and a safe place in which to be your authentic self is so critical for our happiness, not only in childhood but throughout our lives.

Being *Curious* is about valuing the child's experience and wanting to know how it is from the child's perspective. You show curiosity by making time to be with them, talking to them, noticing their emotional state and wondering about their view of the world. It shows in an attitude of being interested in what the child is doing and asking about it ('That looks like an interesting game, where is that car going?', 'I like that drawing, can you tell me about it?') or reflecting on their thoughts or feelings ('You look tired. Did you have a tricky day at school?', 'Why do you think she said that?'). These questions develop critical thinking, empathy and theory of mind skills that help us build healthier relationships and understand other people and ourselves better. This curiosity might involve actually asking the child about why they are behaving or reacting in a particular way or, where they are not able to explain, making some guesses to help the child form into words those links between past experiences and present behaviours. This is something we will come back to in more detail later in the book, as it is very bound in with the final core skill on the list – *Empathy*.

Being *Empathic* is quite challenging, as it means really appreciating and understanding what the experience must have been like for your child and conveying that to them. You might speak aloud what you think their experience is and what from the past that might relate to. For example, you might say, 'It seems like it is really hard for you when I tell you how wonderful you are. I'm sorry if this is not something you've been told much before you came here.' Or you might say, 'You seem really angry that I've asked you to turn the television off. I wonder if you think I told you to do that because I wanted to spoil your fun?' Provided you do it appropriately and not in a way that will overwhelm the child or place blame at the feet of people they feel loyal to, you can also show your own feelings about the child's experiences, such as your sadness about all the things they missed out on and your anger at the people who treated them badly. It is not authentic to try to be emotionally neutral with a child who has just disclosed an awful experience.

To be *Loving* is about showing the child that you enjoy and value them and are able to provide nurture and empathy. As well as showing physical affection, and telling the child that you love them, this can involve spending time together, finding mutual joys and jokes. It can be saying that you missed them or thought about them whilst you were apart. It can also be part of the routine, built in to each day to cement the message. One common way to do that is in the evening when winding down to sleep with a story or a song, tucking them in with a kiss on the head, and wishing them sweet dreams. Whilst having a bedtime routine is something that is mostly associated with younger children, love between parent and child is something that is important throughout our lives. Saying goodnight before going up to bed, and offering hugs when parting or reunifying after time apart, can be habits sustained as the child gets older, and even into adulthood. The practical delivery of love is also embodied by the other letters in the acronym. If it is hard to express love directly, or for the child to receive love directly, you can leave notes or messages, use texts or emojis, or even make a code. For example, writing down a numbered list of phrases like 'I missed you', 'I love you' and 'Even though I told you off, nothing you do could make me love you less' means that you can say 'number four' and they can say 'number four back at you', even in front of their friends! I also heard a lovely story about a mum who drew a circle she called a kiss button on her son's wrist, and said if he pressed the button she would feel it and blow him a kiss to make him feel better. She would then check in each day, telling him how she felt him press the button and sent him a kiss, and asked if he felt her love arrive. She would explain how he must have bumped his wrist if he hadn't intended to press the button!

Case example: Smile over the sadness

Soon after I trained with Dan Hughes, I returned to the UK and was asked to complete an assessment of a teenage girl who had climbed over a safety railing with the intention of jumping off a car park. I asked her all the standard questions about her history and the circumstances of the event and filled in the risk assessment document as normal. She told me that she had decided she might as well be dead after her mother and stepfather had yet another argument. At the end of the explanation, she added 'but, you know' and shrugged and smiled. I said 'I don't know how that is, can you tell me about it?' and she narrated how her drunk stepfather had sworn at her mother, thrown his dinner plate at her across the room and then started hitting her mother, who had retreated with her to the bedroom and locked the door. The stepfather had then charged the door, breaking the lock, and tipped the bed over on top of them. He had picked up a broken bed leg and started to hit her mother with it. Again, the narrative ended with 'but, you know' and a shrug with a smile. I paused for a while and tried to imagine what it must be like to be 14 and to be in fear of your life and your mother's life, whilst a large, angry drunk man beats her in front of you. I felt this overwhelming sense of sadness that anyone should have to experience such a thing. I said to her 'I'm trying to imagine how that must feel, and I just feel so sad that it's trying to leak out of me, whilst you are trying to smile', and a tear literally escaped as if on cue. The girl looked at me and said 'Yeah, it's shit isn't it?' and started to cry. The experience was a profound one for both of us. For her, she knew I understood her experience and was authentically there with her and believing her. For me, I felt like I'd skipped to session 20 of the therapy relationship in which we could have tackled the big issues, safe that the relationship was established.

When we think about how to apply braver empathy to the issues around looked after and adopted children, the same kind of approach can apply. Dan Hughes teaches parents to make very brave guesses about what a behaviour might mean but do so with a playful and accepting tone. One example he told when I trained with him was of two brothers who had been adopted after very serious neglect. The older boy, who had been placed at about the age of four or five, was very used to looking after the younger boy, who had been placed at about the age of 18 months, and he found it extremely difficult in the adoptive home to see the adoptive parents looking after his younger brother.

Dan Hughes described how he did a session with the boy and his parents as a family, where he acted out being playful and curious and empathic about what was causing that situation to be challenging. He said to the boy, 'I've been talking to your mum and dad and they said that it seems to be difficult for you when they care for your brother. I've been wondering about how come it is so hard for you to see them looking after your little brother. I'm just wondering about whether it's because you felt like that was your job. It was one thing that you had to do to keep you busy and that you were good at and felt good about, and now that has been taken away.' The kid shook his head. So Dan Hughes said, 'Oh gosh, well that's a tricky problem. I'm going to have to figure this out a bit more.' So he thought about it for a while and he said to the boy, 'You know, I'm wondering if it could be that your job of looking after your brother made you feel like you were really close to your brother, like he and you were together against the world and he was the person you felt closest to. And now it's really difficult to see your mum and dad getting close to him and it feels like maybe you're being pushed a bit further away.' The boy shook his head.

Dan Hughes said, 'Oh well, this really is a tricky problem! I'm going to have to rack my brains about this one. Do you think we are clever enough to figure it out between us? Come on, I'm smart and you are smart, let's think. Could it be that you felt like your brother really needed you and he was someone that really relied on you and that made you feel responsible and important in the world, but now he's learning to rely on other people and it seems like nobody needs you as much?' Again, the kid shook his head. Dan Hughes said, 'Gosh, this is really difficult! How are we going to solve this? So, you used to look after your brother and did a really good job of that...' The boy interrupted him by shaking his head. Dan Hughes said, 'Oh, now I'm finally getting it. You looked after your brother and you did the best job that you could and you thought that was what your brother needed, but now you see your mum and dad looking after him you realise how a kid should be looked after and that what you were doing for him wasn't enough.' The boy started crying, and the mum and dad started crying, because they were in the room to hear it, and all of us who were on the training were probably crying to hear the story because it was so touching and authentic and emotionally raw.

The reason that the story is really important and I retell it within my groups is because of the fact that Dan Hughes made a number of wrong guesses. And that's the nature of guesses; they will sometimes be wrong. It's a really good illustration of how a child would have experienced people making wrong guesses. This is important to explore because we're not very brave, we don't like to make guesses until we are sure that they are right. But think about how that kid would have felt about Dan Hughes' wrong guesses. Do you think he would have thought 'That stupid man knows nothing about me' or do you think he would have thought 'This person is really trying to understand'? I'd say the child is much more likely to experience the latter. And if he's thinking that someone is really trying to understand him, then Dan Hughes has the tone right, because he is being curious, he's being accepting, he's being empathic and the child's experience is that someone really cares, is interested and is helping him make sense of that experience.

Whilst trying to understand, Dan didn't impose his own opinions. He made it clear that the boy had the final say in whether he was right or not. If a child says he is wrong or has misunderstood, Dan accepts that. We need to take care to be tentative in our guesses so that the child can put us right and we never interfere with their memories (or risk creating false memories by offering guesses that are forceful or prescriptive). Every wrong guess teaches us something about the child's experience, and demonstrates to the child that we are curious about their experience, and empathic to their experiences. The child sees us seeking a shared truth, and wanting to connect with them. When Dan gets the right explanation, the boy is very validated by that being an explanation that someone else can understand. It is then a great opportunity for some empathy and comfort to be offered. When a guess about something as emotionally important as this is correct, it is a very powerful experience for everyone involved.

Certainly, in my groups for foster and adoptive parents, we try to encourage people to be braver in the guesses that they make in order to try and understand the experience of their child. Initially, people are quite anxious about trying that out, but when they do, they find it incredibly rewarding because when you do get the guess right, you feel a closeness and a genuine connection that you may not yet have experienced with the child.

ACTIVITY: EMPATHIC GUESSES

Now that you have read about the idea of empathy and making braver empathic guesses, I would really encourage you to try taking it into practice. Good times for empathy are when the child mentions their past, is self-critical or shows any negative emotions (sadness, anger). Do not try it whilst the child is dysregulated, because of what we have learned about the areas of the brain that are de-activated when the child is in fight or flight mode – to make use of these verbal, reflective techniques we need the frontal part of the brain to be available. So if there is a big outburst, you may need to practise the soothing techniques I mentioned in Chapter 9 until the child is calm and then try some deeper empathy.

The most important thing you can do to show empathy is never to dismiss the child's view of themselves. So, if the child calls themselves stupid, bad, worthless or any other name, resist the Punch and Judy line of 'Oh no, you're not' and the phrases that some of us have been trained into, like saying, 'You are not a bad child. It's just your behaviour that is unacceptable.' Those phrases (unintentionally) close down a really important opportunity for connection with the child. Instead, try imagining how it feels to be that child and to believe that you are bad as a fundamental truth about yourself, and see if you can find a way to express that you empathise with the child's perspective. Although it will feel uncomfortable to stay with empathy and not immediately move to adding something hopeful or attempting to problem solve, it is really valuable for the child to feel understood and accepted. So, try to say things like 'I'm sorry that you feel that way. It must be hard for you to believe that about yourself. It's brave of you to tell me that you feel that way. Thank you for trusting me enough to share that. I'm sad that your life experience has taught you that about yourself' before offering a little of your own perspective to show that there might be a different way of seeing things; for example, 'I hope that one day you are able to see some of the good things about you that I see.'

Don't be disheartened if these beliefs seem resistant to change. Shifting your beliefs about yourself, others and the world takes a lot of time, especially if you have formed those beliefs early on in your life before you were able to think critically about whether they were true, but also if your subsequent life experiences have reinforced them. Abusers can often distort the truth about every aspect of individuals, relationships and the world until it is hard to differentiate fact from fiction. They can be very powerful personalities that shape the behaviours and beliefs of everyone around them. Coercive and controlling individuals can blame their victim each time they maltreat them, cut them off from healthier relationships, and persuade them that they are dependent on their abuser or that the abusive way they are behaving is loving. Children can be persuaded that sexualised behaviour, or exposure to pornography or adult sexual activity, is normal. Or that repeated or sadistic punishments are appropriate to respond to their misbehaviour and done for their own good.

Looking back at my own experiences, I've reflected that some of what seemed at the time like normal teenage boy behaviours, that were a socially acceptable way for them to show their interest in me (and portrayed in my peer group as something I should be flattered by), were actually quite inappropriate – unwanted, overly persistent and at times clearly non-consensual. With the benefit of hindsight,

I have wondered why I didn't recognise this or respond more negatively at the time, and whether this subconsciously motivated my subsequent weight gain (to make myself less attractive, and less easy to push around). But it has taken time and distance for me to gain a more objective perspective, and to internalise more feminist beliefs.

From these relatively small examples in my own life, I have gained a new respect for the task of reprocessing past experiences for those who have lived through abuse and trauma. If a tiny piece of new information, or a new way of looking at things, can throw my certainty about my past experiences into doubt and demand a high emotional load to process, how much more demanding it must be for those whose lives were impacted by much more serious or sustained experiences such as childhood sexual abuse, grooming or coercive control in a relationship. If they have been told they were the problem, or were scapegoated or rejected, that gives a very powerful message that the child internalises as fact. It takes time and effort to reprocess their own story when they are no longer in the sway of the person who is normalising the abuse, but they also have to have the emotional resources and be developmentally ready to do so.

To change the beliefs we have formed starts with acknowledging the experience and exploring the story we have internalised about it. If this is gently challenged, with empathy, it can slowly change. However, beliefs about ourselves, others and the world can be deeply entrenched, and so (as I mentioned in Chapter 11) the process of change is much slower than changing our patterns of thinking and behaviour. Nonetheless, whilst it can be challenging, that reprocessing of experience over time and with greater information is a core part of personal growth (and a key foundation of critical thinking and the scientific method – that as we understand the facts better, we look again at our working hypotheses and adjust them to fit the new information). Understanding ourselves better can help us reach greater happiness and self-actualisation, and also helps us to understand our place in relationships with others, and in the wider world. I see it as a key part of the journey towards both happiness and wisdom.

CHAPTER 13

Layers

If a child mentions a past trauma, no matter what feelings this evokes in you, do not hesitate to discuss it further. Talking about and making sense of these overwhelming experiences helps your child to process them. We are often told not to show the child our feelings as an adult or professional, but (as I mentioned in the case example 'Smile over the sadness' in the last chapter) my training with Dan Hughes and my clinical experience has challenged that. Provided that you can remain regulated (stay in a state that you are not overwhelmed by emotion and are using all of your brain) and do so with empathy for the child, showing some of your feelings can be a positive thing. Seeing that you feel angry with someone who has treated them badly, or sad about their past experiences, can be really helpful in showing the child that their experiences were not acceptable or universal, and can help to deepen the connection with the child. Your emotions are often easier to trust for the child than your words, as they are harder to fake. However, not all children feel able to express all of their past experiences (and what they have learnt to believe about themselves because of them) openly or directly. This can be very confusing, as the child may seem very different in different situations or with different people, or small events may provoke a big reaction. This is something we will come back to in Chapter 17, as it may also reflect 'time holes'.

I often draw Russian dolls as a metaphor for the way we are as people: we have lots of different layers that we only reveal as people get to know us better. In Doodle 20 I have drawn a set of Russian dolls stacked inside each other. The outer layer represents the face we show to the world, so it normally involves trying to show ourselves at our best. In Russian dolls the outer layer is typically the one that is the most decorated, the most painted, the most attractive, so I call that layer 'painted perfect'. It's the mask you want the world to see. In my case that might be trying to appear knowledgeable, organised, professional, intelligent, punctual, friendly or kind. This is how I would like people to perceive me, even though several of these qualities are not things that come naturally to me. (As you'll know if you've seen me arrive for something at the very last minute!) What we choose to show others might be slightly different in different contexts but I think it is a helpful metaphor to think of the outer layer of the Russian dolls as the face that you want other people to see.

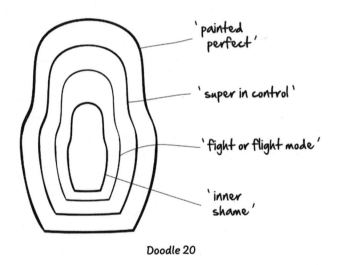

'painted perfect'

'super in control'

'fight or flight mode'

'inner shame'

Doodle 20

Deep inside the Russian doll there is often a sleeping baby doll, which is the least well formed, least attractive, least decorated figure, and in this metaphor that represents the beliefs you learnt about yourself when you were a baby. Those are the very early beliefs about the nature of yourself, the world and other people, which we discussed in Chapter 11 when we looked at formulation. Cognitive behavioural therapists call these 'schemas', and narrative therapists call them story scripts, but they are what you believe are the rules by which the world operates, and they underlie everything you think or feel or do. Remember that before the age of seven children absorb what adults tell them as if it is a fact, with no capacity to consider whether it is true or not or weigh up the evidence for themselves. So if they have heard 'You are a horrible brat' or 'You made me do this' or 'I wish I never had you' or 'This is what you deserve' that is what they will believe as a core truth about themselves – that they are bad, unlovable and deserve maltreatment. This is then reinforced by every subsequent negative message or criticism. Often for children who have been neglected and abused, instead of understanding that they were as wonderful and deserving of love as any other child, and that their maltreatment shows the flaws in their parent/s, their core belief at this level is that they are a bad kid, that they deserve to be (and will inevitably be) treated badly and that the world is full of dangerous people. Their experiences are then understood in the context of that underlying belief, so any maltreatment is seen as evidence that they are broken or unworthy. Experiences like other caregivers who do not harm them, or people who are kind to them, are explained away as the exception to the rule or as not having seen the true nature of the child. This leads to other related beliefs like 'If people knew the real me, I would be abused or rejected', which are very common in this group, though the exact words are different from person to person. Core beliefs like this – which see the source of their negative experiences as being their inherent nature as a bad child – are known as shame and we will talk more about this in the next chapter.

Going back to the Russian dolls metaphor, between the face you want to show to the world (on the outside) and that core hidden set of beliefs you learnt as a baby (on the inside) are the layers that act as your defences against the world. For most young people who have been through trauma, abuse or neglect, the desire is to put on a socially pleasing front, to look attractive, to play the clown or to desperately try to act like their peers at school. So this becomes their outside layer, the one they want you to see. However, this feels quite fragile, rather than authentic, so when they are under any stress you get to see a different facet of their personality – a deeper layer in their Russian doll.

Normally, the one that shows first is what I call 'super in control'. It's a strong desire to take control over the details, to have some say over what other people do, to make life predictable and safe. That is really rational, given the experience many such young people have had of a chaotic, unpredictable life in which the adults were not able to provide any sense of order, organisation or safety. However, it tends to have a sense of an implicit threat to it, as if the message conveyed is: 'Do it my way, or else.' This layer says 'If things go my way they'll be just fine, but just you watch out if they don't!' and so it is unsurprising that the next layer is often an aggressive and/or rejecting layer. This layer is where the child is starting to get really fearful of rejection or maltreatment and covers it up with a tough, fearless presentation. It says, 'I'll hate you before you hate me, I'll reject you before you reject me.' This layer may show all the fight-or-flight skills that the child has learned to survive the chaos and threats they have experienced. They may lash out, be verbally or physically aggressive or threatening, destroy property, or it may lead to the child running away in panic.

Inside that layer, as you reach the innermost layer of the Russian dolls, you get the raw emotions and beliefs from early childhood that normally spill out only when the fight-or-flight neurochemicals are burnt off. This is where you get to see how sad the child feels and how lost and hopeless. They might express that sense of shame, of being a bad and unlovable person and of expecting maltreatment or rejection. This is the child at their most vulnerable, and it is the point at which empathy and non-verbal connection through touch – especially hugs or a cuddle if they will let you – can connect with that vulnerable and developmentally younger part of the child that so desperately needs the love they feel they don't deserve.

Many of the young people I see try to be nice kids, well-behaved kids, someone who is charming or pretty or entertaining – in short, to be what they think others expect them to be (or would want them to be), to act as though they deserve good care and are loveable. However, it doesn't feel authentic. It feels like an act, or a superficial mask that covers what they think of as the truth about themselves, which is full of shame. Under stress they find that mask really difficult to sustain so they become very controlling and want to organise things, even things that are not terribly meaningful; they want the same breakfast bowl, they want to sit in the same place or they want their foster mum to do things in a particular way and in a particular order. If that does not work, or if they feel at all criticised or challenged, they come out with the next defence: being very aggressive and rejecting. They enter that fight-or-flight mode that is really about survival and isn't very logical. All of that masks these inner beliefs about being a bad kid that they desperately want to hide.

Obviously, from individual to individual, there may be differences in how these layers present. I've met children who show nothing but anger, as if they have given up on trying to present a pleasing mask to the world. I've also met young people who don't express any anger, as if showing authentic feelings is just too threatening. I've met young people for whom the outer layer is charming, or babyish, or fashionable, or funny, or intellectual. However, it is remarkable how much common ground there is in the overall pattern. Certainly, I have shared this diagram with a number of young people (such as teenagers who are testing out risk taking and rebelling from their adoptive or foster families to see if they can find a sense of more authentic belonging by seeking out the patterns of their family of origin) and there has been a surprisingly strong response to it. I have several times been told by the young person 'That's it, the thing I can't put words to, that's how I feel' and later been told by the family that this image of Russian dolls has allowed them as a family to talk about the issue that they now see underlies everything they are going through.

Case example: Painted perfect

I worked with a young woman of 16 whose adoptive family were really having difficulties because she was rebelling against their norms and testing out a lot of behaviours that they felt were very risky. For example, she was having some quite unsafe sexual relationships and experimenting with drugs and alcohol and staying out overnight. The referral was triggered because she was doing a number of things that caused concern to her adoptive parents, who then wanted to make restrictive rules and consequences for her. This was a girl who presented absolutely immaculately with the trendiest hairstyle, make-up and nails, and the most fashionable handbag, shoes and styling. She looked immaculate because she was putting so much effort into her external presentation to try and feel a sense of belonging, but actually her inner core belief was that she was maltreated for a reason and didn't deserve this new life. She felt she was maltreated because there was something bad or different about her that she was constantly trying to hide from her adoptive family and friends. That belief was underlying a lot of her experimenting as to whether she deserved a worse life. She was testing out whether letting go of being perfect would allow her to feel more authentic, and whether people would accept her as a whole if the expectations weren't that she should be painted perfect.

In our first session I drew the Russian dolls and asked whether it was something she could identify with. She came back to the next session and her parents said, 'She's finally got some words to talk about how she is feeling.' The parents were able to work on giving empathy to the inner beliefs she was hiding, and she was able to show some more authentic fears to her parents. It did not have an immediate impact on her risky behaviour, but, with continued empathy, she realised that she felt more of a sense of belonging in her adoptive family when following their norms of expected behaviour than she did when hanging out with more chaotic peers and acting like the stories she was told about her family of origin.

I also think the Russian dolls are a useful metaphor in terms of the idea of needing to accept the child as a whole. Most people I know who have gone into fostering or adoption want to love that child despite, or even because of, all of the difficult experiences that child has had, and have a sincere desire to help them recover. They take on the child in the knowledge of all of their experiences, and the fact that the child has been harmed by them and is likely to present in ways that are challenging because of them. They don't have an expectation of a perfect child. Yet most of the children I know in those same families are very ashamed of those difficult experiences and want to hide them and pretend never to have had them. They believe that they don't deserve the love of their new family, or the improved quality of life that they are being given, and that if their new parents knew the truth about them, they wouldn't love or accept them. This makes the new living arrangement feel very precarious to the child – and this feeling can become stronger and more anxiety provoking as they start to enjoy their new life or feel affection towards their new caregivers.

Although there are a great range of circumstances and stories that bring children into Care, in my experience families where children are taken into Care tend to be more socioeconomically deprived than adoptive and foster families, and may not have the same standards of cleanliness or abundance of material possessions that adoptive and foster families can offer. Many children have grown up in homes that are smaller, more crowded and much less child-centred than the ones they are later placed in. All the homes where they have visited friends or family members may also be similar to that of their birth family, and they may never have seen homes where each child has their own bedroom, or where there is plenty of space to play, well-stocked food cupboards or a choice of books, toys or art materials. They may never have been given new clothes, presents or a birthday party. They can therefore feel out of place in the new home, or believe that they don't deserve this new lifestyle. The stronger their sense of shame, the stronger this sense of not belonging somewhere too nice can feel.

The same can be true of relationships. Their expectation of 'normal' could be that adults mostly ignore them, and criticise them if they express any needs. They might not have experienced any physical affection like hugs or kisses or being tucked up in bed at night. They may never have been rocked or sung a lullaby as infants. They may never have been read a book or told a story. They may not have been shown how to do things, engaged in shared play activities or cooking or sat down as a family to talk and eat meals together. They may not have heard praise when they were trying hard or did things well. Yet for the foster or adoptive parent, those things can be the bread and butter of how they expect to care for a child. This mismatch of expectations can mean that the child feels that things are too nice, or better than they deserve, especially if they are filled with blame and shame.

This can be a barrier to communication, particularly if the adult is giving praise or affection which the child is not used to, as the child's world view is that they don't deserve that. The adult's behaviour feels confusing as it doesn't fit with their past experience, so instead of rethinking their established beliefs the child is likely to think that this particular adult hasn't yet realised what kind of person they are (which they believe to be bad and undeserving of love, praise or nice things). So what you get is a child who, whenever they are praised, is at some level thinking, 'Hah, I've got them fooled with my painted perfect mask' and doesn't believe the compliment to be genuine to them. But whenever you criticise them, even about the most minor thing, the child is thinking 'Oh shit, they've seen the true me and I might be rejected. They've realised I'm a bad kid and now I'm going to be maltreated.' That's really difficult because it means that all the affection, kindness and effort that carers are putting in to help show the good qualities of that child to them are just being brushed off as being false. Praise is just attributed to the surface layer and doesn't sink in, and the slightest hint of negative in any feedback they give to help shape that child to achieve the best possible outcomes in life is seen as criticism that cuts them to the core.

As I said earlier, Dan Hughes talks about how whenever the child reveals a belief about themselves being bad or says anything self-critical, this is a great opportunity for connection and empathy. Whenever you hear the child describe feelings of shame, deflect praise or overreact to criticism you need to be very empathic by saying things like: 'I'm sorry to hear you think that you are a bad kid. That must be really difficult for you. It's brave of you to tell me that you feel like that. I'm really sad that your life experiences before you came to us made you feel like that about yourself.' The risk in a Supernanny-style response, like saying 'No, no, you're not bad, it's just the behaviour that is unacceptable', is that the child would hear this message as 'Don't tell me about your inner core beliefs, just keep acting like the painted perfect layer', which means that they continue to feel that their true self is unacceptable to you. To disagree with their belief is also to tell them that the way they perceive the universe is wrong. That would be like me pointing to the sky and saying it's orange; it just doesn't make any sense, so it makes the child think that you're stupid and doesn't help them understand that because of their skewed experience they are seeing things differently from the objective truth. It is much more effective to acknowledge the child's perspective as legitimately reflecting their experience, to accept the child where they are with the beliefs they currently hold, to connect this with their past experiences and then (if you feel the need to end on a positive note) to offer an alternative interpretation as a possibility.

A core skill in being able to show deep empathy is really accepting the child's point of view as being legitimate given their experiences, even if they think they are a bad kid and they deserve be treated badly. You might notice shame when the child says something outright that is self-critical, but it might also be that they dismiss a compliment or avoid eye contact and appear uncomfortable at certain times. Interestingly, we avoid eye contact when we are both ashamed of what someone might see in us or really worried about what we might see in them. So the child may find it nearly impossible to look at you if you tell them off, as they fear that you have seen the badness inside them and would hate or reject them. But they might also find it very hard to look at you if they think you are being too positive about them when offering praise, affection or hope, because they believe that if they look into your eyes either you or they will see that this is a lie. I would never recommend that you force the child to make eye contact with you – in fact this could be quite emotionally abusive for a traumatised child. But it can be helpful to prompt the child to check your face to see if they think you mean what you say at times they seem sceptical about your honesty, as (although negative past experiences can make you interpret facial expressions and tone of voice more negatively) most people are intuitively sensitive to reading other people's emotional states and level of readiness for fight or flight.

Finding the right balance between accepting the child as they are and allowing them to express their beliefs, and gently challenging them to look at you to check how you are feeling, is one of the skills in sensitive re-parenting. We cannot make our body language and the subtler parts of our facial expression lie, so it can be really helpful to encourage the child to have a really good look at you when you say you love them, or that the fact they did something wrong doesn't mean you are going to reject them, to see if they can make a better judgement of whether it is sincere or fake.

You will become an expert in your child and know their body language, their behaviour and their beliefs. This will allow you to learn when empathy is appropriate. But starting with believing their world view is the mark of true acceptance and empathy, and it will gradually allow the child to tell you more and more about their experience. The more you can spot these moments with the potential for deepening your connection and offer a sincere experience of empathy, the more understood the child feels and the more their shame becomes something that can be talked about and shared, rather than hidden for fear of rejection. True empathy can be really difficult for us as adults because it brings up a lot of strong feelings (including overwhelming feelings of sadness or anger about what the child has been through, or it can resurface feelings about your own past experiences). There may be a strong instinct to move on quickly to problem solving or discussing something more positive. As I mentioned earlier, after the empathy it can be helpful to add a few of your own thoughts about the qualities that you see in the child, and to hope that one day the child can also recognise these. If the feelings that come up for you are particularly strong, it can be helpful to talk about these with a trusted confidant like a partner or friend, or if they feel particularly personal or overwhelming this can be a really good reason to speak to a therapist who knows about attachment and trauma.

As I mentioned above, the Russian doll layers that I draw are just an example of what might be there. They might be in a slightly different order for different people, or it might be that the outer layer is painted like a clown or like a very young or ill child who needs a lot of nurture (which we'll come back to in Chapter 18), or it might be that the defences come in a different order, or there are more of them before you reach the vulnerable inner shame. However, the idea of the outer layers being presented in order to get your needs met in a particular way whilst the negative core beliefs are hidden is the important aspect of this image. I hope that by thinking about the layers that particular children might present, foster and adoptive carers can start to recognise them in real life and respond with greater empathy and acceptance. One of the really core concepts of how to do therapeutic re-parenting is to recognise what these inner beliefs mean, where they come from and what you can do about them, and that leads us on to the idea of shame.

💡 Reflection: Spotting the layers

Take some time to think about your child. What would they want to convey about themselves to their friends, their school, a visitor or you? What role are they most comfortable in? What would they want to hide? How do they respond to praise? How do they respond to criticism? Have they ever said anything self-critical or talked about their past experiences? What might they have learned to believe about themselves?

CHAPTER 14

Shame and Changing the Norm

In the last chapter, we talked about the fact that a child's early experiences lead them to have certain beliefs about themselves, which often equate to them being a bad person who is unworthy of love and good experiences. This is a very powerful set of beliefs that completely change a child's self-image and the way they view the world. I think Dan Hughes explains shame really well. He draws a shield shape and uses it to illustrate the defences that indicate underlying shame, which is the basis for Doodle 21. He talks about how if a person with underlying shame feels criticised at all, they will tend to deny what they have done as the first defence, then minimise it, then blame it on someone or something else, and then go into rage – getting disproportionately angry. The rage could also be thought of as the activation of fight-or-flight defences; the final defence in the Russian dolls we talked about in the previous chapter.

Case example: Hitting out

I can think of an example of a session in which I talked to a child called Chloe who hit her cousin, seemingly without provocation, during a family get-together. I asked, 'Why did you hit your cousin?' Chloe responded, 'I never. I never hit her.' (That's denial.) I said, 'Well, you know what, I was talking to your mum and dad and they're pretty reliable people and they saw you hit her, so I'm thinking that you did hit her.' 'Well, I didn't hit her very hard, it wasn't a proper hit, she's just a cry-baby.' (That's minimising.) 'Well, you know what? You made your cousin cry and your mum and dad said it looked pretty hard, so I think we probably ought to talk about what's going on with this hitting.' 'Well, it's her fault. She poked me four times but my mum and dad never see that. They say she's little and so it doesn't count what she does to me. They love her better. They said they wanted a girl like her that was well behaved. They don't care about me. I hate them, they always take her side. I hate her, and I hate them. I wish I was never born.' That's gone straight from blame into rage and shame and jealousy, and that's when it explodes, which was what the parents had described to me.

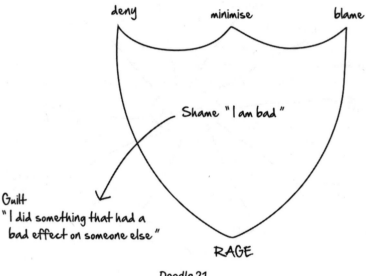

deny   minimise   blame

Shame "I am bad"

Guilt
"I did something that had a
bad effect on someone else"

RAGE

Doodle 21

Dan Hughes would say that going around the shield of shame is a big red flag for the fact that the child is holding core beliefs around being bad. Shame is a belief along the lines of: 'I'm bad, I deserve to be treated badly.' If a child is overwhelmed by shame, that becomes the reason for everything they do: 'Why did you hurt your friend?' 'Because I'm a bad kid.' 'Why did you break that?' 'I'm a bad kid.' It becomes the answer to everything and there is no motivation to change; there is no hope that one day life could be better, as the reason for life being bad in their belief system is that they deserve it because of some innate qualities. But being overwhelmed with shame is also an egocentric position; it is all about looking inward and blaming yourself, and there isn't any empathy for other people or awareness of the consequences of your actions on others. It is a very immature stage of social development, which children normally pass through in the first two years of life. What we need to do as parents, carers and therapists is to help a child to move from shame towards guilt. Guilt is an outward-facing understanding of what you have done wrong, which demonstrates empathy to others. It says 'What I did had a bad effect on someone else', and it recognises behaviour as a choice rather than the inevitable acting out of innate characteristics. That position motivates people to change their behaviour, because they are able to see they have some control and they are suddenly aware of (and ideally caring about) the outcome for others.

This means that one of the times that empathy is at its most effective is when you see shame. As soon as a child does anything that suggests they believe that they are bad or that leads to denial, minimisation, blame or rage, those are the times that we need to find ways of being empathic. Those are the times that we need to be able to regulate our own arousal levels enough to come back with empathy rather than annoyance (dysregulation) ourselves. That can be challenging if the child is misbehaving in a way that has a negative impact on you, other children or your environment – and it can be particularly socially challenging if they do so in front of other people or in public. They may have learnt exactly the things that press your buttons to trigger a negative response or the situations in which you find it difficult to respond in a consistent way. They may also be able to trigger surprisingly strong feelings in you, which is something we will come back to in Chapter 18 when talking about patterns that suck you in. But for all these reasons, emotions might be running high, and empathy may not be the response that is easiest to respond with. That means that we need to use our support network (the 'tag team' I mentioned earlier) to take over whenever we begin to feel very angry or to have strong chaotic negative feelings.

Some people ask about whether empathy should be given instead of consequences for behaviour, and if so whether the child will feel that they are being rewarded for their misbehaviour or being allowed to get away with things that are unacceptable. I believe that the ideal response is a mixture of both empathy and consequences. If these are in balance, you are at your most effective as a parent (see Doodle 22). If all you give is empathy, the child's past becomes their excuse for everything they do and change is not necessary. If all you offer are consequences, the child's shame is reinforced; they feel like a bad kid and they feel like there is no motivation to change. But if you combine empathy with consequences, you can help the child to understand where the behaviour is coming from, why they do it, why it's not okay and how they can change. That is the best of all possible outcomes.

Doodle 22

It's making that link between past experience and present behaviour that is really important in allowing change to be possible. Dan Hughes uses what I call brave empathic guesses to start offering empathy at times when the child is showing shame. So, for example, if a child struggles when you tell them to turn off the television and starts becoming destructive and full of rage, you might say, 'I know it's really frustrating to turn off the television when you are watching something you want to. I guess that it might be if you've had a life like yours where you didn't get to do so many fun things and the people who interrupted you doing fun things were being mean. I can see why you would find that frustrating. I'm sorry that it makes you feel that way. But you know what, when you are a mum, sometimes you have to turn off the television and get the child to do other things so they can learn. Because I love you and want a really good life for you, I really am going to have to keep doing this, even though I know it's frustrating for you.' Every time you have that conversation, you are linking the child's feelings to their behaviour, but you are also linking the child's feelings to where they may have come from in their past experience, so it's a really powerful way of applying empathy.

When you give consequences with empathy, the child is often more able to accept them. For example, in the case example above about Chloe, the child who hit her cousin, a therapist trained in Dyadic Developmental Psychotherapy might go on to say, 'Oh, if you feel like your parents don't love you as much as they love your cousin, no wonder you feel so angry with her. That would feel so unfair. I'm wondering if when you lived with your birth mum it felt like that too – that your older sister was much more important and you felt like you got left out of the good stuff and told off much more than her. That would be a horrible thing for you to go through, if you were not treated as nicely as your sister. I'm sorry you experienced that, and I hope that I can help your mum and dad to show you better how much they love you and see good things about you. But you know what? It's still not okay to hit your cousin, so I think you should do something to make it up to her. How about you say sorry to her and play that game that she likes this afternoon?'

The other important thing when considering the balance of empathy and consequences is to be aware (as I mentioned in Chapter 4) that the child might be unconsciously recreating negative experiences and sabotaging positive experiences. So it might be necessary for you to recognise that pattern and disrupt it. For example, you might say, 'I know that I said you needed to be good this week in order to go to the party on Friday. Well, it seems like we've had a terrible week, and I wonder if part of you felt like you didn't deserve to go to the party. I could keep you at home, but I think you've had enough experience of missing out on nice things, so I've decided that it is more important for you to go to the party and have fun.' Or you might say, 'It seems to me like you are trying to make me angry today. I'm a bit fed up of being angry, so let's try and do something different today. How about we go out to the park or get an ice cream?' Some psychologists would call these paradoxical responses, which is a way of saying that you do the opposite of what is expected.

You might be thinking that this lets the child 'win', as if there is a constant battle for control between parent and child. I wonder if there is a different way to think about this. If you picture a child who keeps speaking back to their teacher, we can all imagine the scene where they are given a detention, and then talk back, so they are given two days of detention, so they talk back and are given a week of detention; this causes them to swear at the teacher, so the detention is then extended to a month, and when they talk back again they are then sent out of the classroom to the head teacher, and they stomp off spitting more profanities as they go. Who wins this game? The teacher has more power in the system, but both are equally keen to get the last word, and the conflict steps up and up without an opportunity for resolution, and probably leaves residual bad feeling in both directions. As a result the child is less likely to engage in future lessons and in education more generally. Each party is trapped in the same game of trying to get the last word. However, there is also the opportunity to take a different path. If the teacher could laugh at the child's first comment ('Seems like you really want me to go for a bigger consequence, but I think we should stick there') or give it some empathy ('Yeah, I'm sure it's frustrating that I picked on you when other people were talking too, but we have rules for a reason and it will give you a chance to finish the work from this lesson') it might not need to step up into a more serious conflict. The real power in this situation is not in who can win the game, but who has the power to change the game. So if there are repeated points of conflict between you and the child, perhaps there is another way you can tackle it, with humour or empathy or a paradoxical response.

Kim Golding[1] reminds us of the value of preserving a positive family atmosphere and actively choosing to take the more enjoyable option so that as a family you are able to have more positive shared

1   See Golding (2008).

experiences. This is important not only for the child, who may have missed out on a lot of normal enjoyable experiences, but also for the family, who also deserve to have positive experiences of being together. It is helpful to find ways to have fun and focus on the positive parts of the relationship, even when the child's behaviour can at times be draining and emotionally exhausting (and seem to keep you in a punitive position as a caregiver, which is something we will return to in Chapter 17).

As I mentioned in the previous chapter, children who are removed from their family of origin and placed into Care or adopted have often had quite emotionally and materially deprived lives within their birth family and have a template of what life is like in a family that does not contain the level of nurture, attention, care and comfort that many of us would consider to be the norm. As the brick-wall activity in Chapter 3 showed, there are often missing experiences or components of 'good enough' care and experiences that were skewed in an unhealthy way, as well as the presence of traumatic and abusive experiences.

Case example: Making the ordinary extraordinary

I went to visit a girl called Elouise in her foster placement about five months after she was removed from her family of origin. I asked her to tell me about what was different in the house. She showed me how they had a garden where they grow some vegetables, and she had her own room with pink bedding. Elouise told me she'd had the 'best ever day out' when her foster carer had taken her to a farm park where they had been able to look at the fish and pets and had stopped for a drink and some cake in the café. The foster carer told me how Elouise had found it almost impossible to be bought new things unless they bought enough that each of her siblings (placed elsewhere) could have one before her. When she saw her siblings, if any of them complimented something she was wearing or had brought with her, she would immediately hand it over to them. Her foster carer learnt to collect back her hair clips, water bottle (and once even her shoes) at the end of the session. When bought a party dress, Elouise had been shaking and crying with delight to try it on, as she had never had anything so pretty and brand new before. She had said to the foster carer, 'I promise I will keep it nice and clean so that when my mummy gives it to my sister she will still think it is a new dress.' It was inconceivable for Elouise to imagine that she deserved something nice in her own right. In her experience, everything in life was rationed and she was the lowest priority – last in the queue after her mother and her four siblings.

I found it really upsetting to hear how such a beautiful kind little girl placed so little value on herself and how she gave away her nicest things and struggled to accept anything for herself. I had to stop my car to have a bit of a cry about it on my way home. But it gave me a very clear sense of how her birth family functioned that I could share with the court.

Elouise was very worried that if she felt or expressed affection towards the foster carer, this would mean that she loved her birth mother less, which would conflict with her fantasy hope in which her mother loved and wanted her and their relationship could be fixed. It was very understandable, as she came from a world where everything, including attention and affection, were in such short supply and not always available – and where she had very low priority in the pecking order for anything nice. I talked to Elouise and her foster carer about how love is not like a cake, where the more people you cut it up for, the less any one person gets. Love is like candles, where the more you light, the more light there is for everyone.

As Elouise stayed in the placement, she began to be able to accept the normality of life in the foster family – that being read bedtime stories, or given medicine when she felt ill, were things that she deserved. The social worker described her as 'opening like a flower' in the new environment, and the court was able to recognise the need for Elouise to be adopted into a family where she could be the centre of attention. She was not placed with her siblings, although regular ongoing contact was arranged.

Similarly, I was really struck by going to hear a talk about Childline, the charity that children can contact if they want to get support or report abuse or distressing experiences. One of their early calls was from a girl who rang up and said, 'I feel really stupid calling, but the other girls in my class tell me that children do not usually sleep on the garage floor on newspaper.'

It really goes to show how strongly normative our own experiences become – that every person believes that their life experiences are commonplace until they start recognising, through broader experiences outside their family of origin, that what they experienced is not how it happens elsewhere. Obviously, this can only happen when you have other experiences to compare and contrast with, and for many children this process only begins when they are removed from their family of origin. Initially they think that the family they are placed in is the exception to the norm and not vice versa. When coupled with a strong sense of shame and not deserving positive experiences, it can be very hard for young people whose whole world was made of experiences that most people would consider to be dysfunctional to re-norm themselves.

☼ Reflection: **Visiting the unfamiliar**
Have you ever visited a different household or a different part of the country (or a different part of the world) and noticed how different the day-to-day sensations are? Think about somewhere you have been that felt different. Was it louder/quieter? Did it smell different? Were there more or fewer people? Did the people behave differently? Did they talk a different language, or with a different accent? Were there different plants or animals around? Was the landscape and colour palette different? How did it make you feel in your body? Were you tenser or more relaxed? Did your feelings change over time? Did anything help you to feel more comfortable?

Hopefully this exercise will help you to think about how it must be for children to change their expectations when they change placements. As I've mentioned previously, many of the children who live outside of their family of origin will have experienced care that fell below the standard of 'good enough'. As well as experiencing abuse or trauma, they have often experienced a chaotic or neglectful home, where there are not the same norms and routines as we might be accustomed to. Think back to Oliver, who at the age of nine had never heard nursery rhymes. Or Elouise who had never had a new dress and thought a day out at a garden centre was the best day ever.

The experiences of childhood that people have vary widely. Some are used to nannies and au pairs, and being packed off to boarding school at a young age. Some have an at-home parent, or a mixture of nursery and parental care. Some people have two parents involved in their care. Some have one. Some have an extended family network. Some have care split between the home and families of separated parents. Different cultures can have different norms for parenting, and these can vary according to where in the world you grow up (e.g., in Kenya 90 per cent, and in Toga, Jordan and the Philippines around three quarters, of parents report having used a form of physical punishment on their child within the last month that would be considered harmful by UK and most international standards[2]). Some people grow up with supportive loving families, others look back on critical, punitive or abusive elements in their childhood, or parents who required us to take on the role of carer, or work around their mental health or drug/alcohol use.

Even for caring families with attentive parents who recognise the needs of their children, their economic situation and lifestyle can impact significantly on the childhood experience. Perhaps parents have to work long hours and spend little time at home. Or perhaps they have to frequently relocate or spend months away from home, such as when having different deployments in the armed forces. Or perhaps they have jobs that require them to spend a lot of time travelling internationally, commuting long distances or locked away in a home office attending online meetings. In those circumstances it can be hard to also meet the psychological needs of children. But

---

2   See Lansford *et al.* (2017), Runyan *et al.* (2010) and Sanapo and Nakamura (2011).

perhaps the biggest challenge is poverty. For those who are the most socially excluded and have the least income (e.g., homeless people, migrants and asylum seekers) this can be a barrier to meeting children's needs at the most basic level, for shelter and warmth, food and hygienic conditions. However, the impact of economic stress has become more of an issue for an increasing number of families as the cost of food and energy has spiralled whilst the value of wages and benefits have not risen proportionately. For many families the costs of rent and bills mean there isn't enough left for food or for heating. Children may not have had breakfast before school, or there may be days when there is not enough left to have a cooked meal in the evening. If they are not entitled to school meals, some children bring empty lunchboxes to school and pretend to have already eaten their packed lunch, so that they are not embarrassed amongst their friends. Some may rely on food banks, or breakfast clubs, or scavenging leftovers. The house may be cold, dark and damp. There may not be the means to launder and dry clothes. Over the last decade, life might not be the same for these children as most of us remember from our own childhoods, when energy and food prices were cheaper, and there was more support available within communities.

If we add in the reasons that the children came into Care, such as abuse, neglect, trauma, domestic violence, parental drug or alcohol misuse, poor state of the home, lack of supervision and a lack of developmentally appropriate stimulation and experiences, we can see that their lives might be very different to the image we have of a typical loving family. The more different the child's template of what normal life is like is from the new life they receive in a placement, the more challenging it will be for them to adjust and feel a sense of belonging in the new place. Yet differences can also mean there are fewer reminders of past traumas (which can trigger strong emotions or behaviours in response, as we will discuss in Chapter 17).

We will look at some strategies to increase a child's sense of belonging in the next few chapters.

CHAPTER 15

Roles and Belonging

Each of us is influenced by a number of societal and family expectations about roles. We have a sense of what is required of us that is determined by our age, our gender, our culture, our religion, our peer group, our profession, our appearance, any disability, neurodivergence, learning need or difference from the norm and numerous other factors. We also have expectations of what it means to have our position within the sibling group (e.g., to be the oldest, the middle child, the baby of the family) but also to have our particular traits or reputations within the family (e.g., to be 'the helpful one', 'the practical one', 'the ditzy one', 'the funny one', 'the naughty one' or 'the clever one'). These roles or stereotypes have a huge influence on how we understand ourselves and anticipate how others will interact with us.

For example, as an older sister, I was brought up believing it was a positive characteristic to look after others, and I learned to be more practical and assertive than my younger brother. Our family strongly valued education and learning. As I grew older people listened to what I had to say, so I started to believe that what I said was interesting. It is no surprise given this context that I remained in education a long time and then went into a 'helping profession' in which I do a lot of talking but can also apply practical skills or assertiveness when necessary! I gained the confidence to assert my opinion and the belief that I needed to work hard to ensure that I was financially independent (which I now associate with my maternal grandmother who was a working single mother before that was a socially acceptable role in her culture, and then remarried unhappily, believing that would give my mum a better life). But I was also taught, perhaps as much by society as by anything explicit in my family, that girls should be kind and accommodating and that male attention should be treated as a compliment and deflected where necessary without hurting the man's feelings. That meant that as a teenager and young adult I put up with male behaviour that I would now see as unacceptable.

Interestingly, the labels that we apply to people easily become a self-fulfilling prophecy. In several scientific studies, pupils' attainments have been shown to be heavily influenced by the expectations of their teachers and parents.[1] If children are selected randomly and flagged to their teacher as having hidden potential, their scores will rise more than those of their peers over the course of the following year. Where we expect children to misbehave, they often fulfil the expectation. Parental expectations and the way parents treat their children are immensely powerful in determining the outcomes for those children.[2] Changing the way parents treat their children changes what these children achieve dramatically, for example the 38 million children who received the Head Start program over the last 60 years.[3]

When we look at children who have been rejected within their family of origin, or blamed for placement breakdowns, we typically see young people with disorganised attachments. Those are the kids with the major behaviour problems, the self-harm, the 'manipulative' and 'attention-seeking' behaviour, the ones who are the most vulnerable to being victims of further abuse and/or criminal or sexual exploitation by predatory adults. The more Adverse Childhood Experiences a person experiences, and the more changes of caregiver and of placement they go through, the more likely they are to have problems that follow them into adulthood. This can mean

---

1 See Davis-Kean (2005) and Rosenthal and Jacobson (1968).
2 Negative parental appraisals lead to an increased chance of the negative behaviour. See Matsueda (1992).
3 Interventions like Head Start make massive change to outcomes. See Mills (1998), U.S. Department of Health and Human Services (HHS) (2022), Welsh and Farrington (2007), Zagar, Busch and Hughes (2009) and Zigler and Muenchow (1994).

they recreate (unintentionally) the very things that have already scarred them in childhood in their adult lives and for their own children. They often hold a strong sense of the chaos and rejection being their fault, and no matter where they go, they take this with them.

When I think about the impact of toxic life experiences on children, I tend to think of an image from the film *Spirited Away* (a Japanese animation by Hayao Miyazaki, from Studio Ghibli) which I think can be a helpful metaphor for a different way of seeing very troubled children. There is a scene in which the main character, a young girl called Sen, is working in a bathhouse for the spirits. A giant stink spirit arrives, illustrated as a huge putrid slug trailing disgusting black gloop, who wants to use the baths. No one is willing to assist him because of the smell, so Sen (who is the lowest ranking employee) is sent in to run the baths. As she runs the water, she notices that the stink spirit appears to have a large splinter. She attaches a rope and helps to pull it out. Out comes a broken bicycle, followed by a boot, some fishing line, a tyre, rusted metal oil barrels and a whole pile of other items of rubbish and pollution until the room is filled. Once the mess and water clears, it becomes apparent that the stink spirit has transformed into an elderly but beautiful river spirit. He had been disguised by years of pollution that had been thrown into the river, but once this is separated from him, he is able to realise his true form again.

I tend to think that a lot of the children I meet have been polluted by their life experiences and are unable to show their full potential because of this. As we treat them well and show them that they deserve a better life, they are able to disclose and sift through all the negative experiences that have changed their sense of self and ways of reacting with others in the safety of a supportive relationship. Gradually, they are able to show us glimpses of their true form – the child they would have been if they had only experienced secure care and positive role models in their life. However, at first they can be very well disguised and good at using their most disgusting learnt qualities to keep people away.

⬦ Reflection: **Roles**

Have a think about the roles that different people in your family took. What influenced your development? What roles did you have to fit in with? What impact has that had on your development? Did you like the roles assigned to you or rebel against them? What was the role of a parent in your experience?

Now think about the role expectations that might have been there for your child in their birth family. What was expected of them? What were their parents like? How were they thought of? How about since they arrived in your family? What role do they take on with you? Is this similar or different to how they interact with other caregivers or adult members of the family? How about with siblings or other children? At school? What labels have they attracted? Do they take on different roles in different contexts? What roles do they like and dislike?

It is interesting to think about whether the role people take on is one of a number of facets of their personality or whether it is the only aspect of them that other people see. I know that when I am in different environments, I show different facets of myself. For example, when people read what I have written for psychology graduates or people training in clinical psychology, I am perceived by them to be a sort of stern and serious character, but if they come to an event where they can meet me or hear me speak, they often comment about me being younger, more cheerful or less scary than they expected! Within my family, I might be perceived as the one who is good at problem solving and helps out other people, but that can make it difficult for others to recognise when I am struggling and could do with a bit of help.

Roles that we take on can be conscious or subconscious. We can intentionally present particular facets of ourselves (e.g., if in a professional role, or entertaining others, or at a job interview, or on a first date) or they can be triggered by the context (e.g., if you feel threatened, or if someone reminds you of someone you have had strong feelings about in the past). We can also be strongly influenced by social expectations. This might be about gender (e.g., for women not to be too assertive or to express any anger or negative emotions, or for men not to show any sign of weakness), religion or culture, or the increasingly polarised political and social attitudes we hold. As I mentioned when we were thinking about Russian dolls, when we meet new people we typically try hard to be pleasing, and to show the best facets of ourselves. If we want to develop that relationship, we normally try to learn how much of our values we have in common, and (if we still like them) we try to judge whether the feelings are reciprocated and they like us. It takes most of us time, and a lot of trust, to show our full authentic selves, complete with our quirks and flaws. But it is only when we show our full selves, and see their full selves, that we can see whether the relationship is genuine and likely to be sustainable. I think that the key marker of love in a relationship is when both parties can be their authentic selves and feel fully accepted and unconditionally liked exactly as they are. That is true in a romantic relationship but also in a parent-child relationship, as we discussed when talking about Dan Hughes' PACE qualities in an earlier chapter.

Some of the roles that the child takes on are associated with the defensive layers we talked about with the metaphor of Russian dolls. They serve a function to protect the child from anxiety – including a perceived risk of rejection if they showed their true selves.

Case example: The naughtiest boy in the naughty boys' club

I worked with a young lad called Ernest who prided himself on being the naughtiest boy in his school and on the estate where he lived. He found it very hard to stay still and often ended up in trouble and getting punished, both at home and at school. He had a list of stories about his adventures and the consequences of these, which he would retell with great relish to anyone who would listen. When Ernest's adoptive parents came to see a colleague and me in clinic, he was unable to stay in the room. He wandered out into the car park, so I followed him and started to talk to him. He seemed somewhat surprised that

I didn't seem to mind that he was outside, and was somewhat baffled when, instead of me telling him off for trying to climb over the wall, I suggested that he try to climb one of the small trees in the planted area adjacent. He was unable to reach the lower branches, so I made him a step up with my cupped hands, and he climbed up and sat on a big branch so his feet dangled down near my face.

I said it was brave of him to trust me to make a step for him, and he acknowledged that he felt I might be trustworthy. I asked him if it was scary to be up high, and he said it was a little bit. I said that lots of people I work with have had experiences that are scary, and Ernest said that he had seen scary things where he lived before. I asked if it was scary where he lived now. He told me that it was a little bit, because his adoptive mum was poorly, and he had been told that the reason he couldn't live with his birth mother was that she was poorly but that people really meant she was using drugs. He was quite worried that his adoptive mother might not be able to look after him and that he didn't quite know what was wrong with her. We made an agreement to go and find out this information.

It transpired that she had recently had a hysterectomy. We were able to talk with Ernest about the differences between what happened to his birth mother because of her drug addiction and what was currently happening to his adoptive mother. I was able to explain about fight or flight and talk about how being 'naughty' felt stronger and safer than being scared. This allowed the adoptive parents to respond to the unexpressed need (anxiety) and offer reassurance, rather than thinking of him as self-sufficient and challenging.

BELONGING

I would also like to think about the idea of belonging, because an adoption or long-term foster placement is like an arranged marriage, where there isn't always an immediate sense of love or fitting together comfortably (though, like arranged marriages, the majority of relationships work out quite well in the end, provided they are approached with the right attitude). Sometimes there is 'love at first sight' but often it is a feeling that grows slowly, and there can be blockages that get in the way, based on the past experiences of either the parent or the child (or the combination of the two).

💡 Reflection: **Belonging**

Think about whether you have ever felt a strong sense of belonging or not belonging in a place or group. Perhaps you have been in a school, team, club or workplace where you felt strongly that you either were or were not a valued part of the group. You may have felt that this changed if you had to move from one school, location or job to another. Did you feel like you fitted in at the new place better, or did you miss the old place? What was different?

Perceived belonging is an incredibly powerful sense we have in different environments as to whether we feel comfortable and at ease, or tense and awkward or able to show only one facet of ourselves. When I run groups for foster and adoptive carers and for professionals, I often get people to think about times in their own lives that they have had a very strong sense of belonging or not belonging. People have talked about particular social clubs, workplaces, communities that they have lived in, adolescent groups that had particular ways of dressing or associated with different musical styles or hobbies, professional groups or being involved in sporting activities or military activities; a whole variety of different examples. We also often discuss moving from one area of the country to another, moving abroad from one country to another or changing schools or workplaces. People often report that they felt more comfortable in one than they did in another. People often report that they felt more comfortable in one scenario than they did in another. These all sound like very varied experiences at first. However, as we discuss them, the examples all seem to boil down to similar core experiences.

When we talk about what gives a sense of belonging, it is often about looking the same as others in the group (perhaps wearing the same uniform or style of clothing), having a common language or accent, similar reference points and figures of speech, and common experiences with other people. The result is feeling that you are like them in some way and that they know you well enough to treat you in a way that you like to be treated. When you belong, you know people's nicknames, you know the shared jokes, you know the story and the history, you feel accepted and things are familiar. You feel safe and as if you have a particular defined role that you feel confident in fulfilling. When people have a strong sense of not belonging, it is often the case that they feel left out of the group because they look or sound different, are not aware of those shared jokes, shared language or nicknames or they feel uncertain of their role or their value to others. They may have experienced teasing for things that are different or felt that people have not recognised their efforts, or they may feel that there are unclear expectations or that they are not known as an individual.

A related idea is whether you feel like you matter to anyone and whether your views matter to those making decisions about you. This appears to be very important in our sense of self and our mental health. The perception of anti-mattering, where you perceive that your views are deliberately ignored, contradicted or overridden, is associated with increased rates of depression and suicidal thinking.

Looked after and adopted children often have a strong sense of not belonging. It is difficult to give a new person an experience of belonging when they come to your home. Unlike the people you have lived with for a long time, you will not know what their favourite breakfast cereal is, whether they are a morning person or an evening person, an outdoor person or a home body, or whether they like to be very social or have a lot of quiet time to themselves. It would be difficult to tell someone the stories and the history of all the names and things that are going on in your household straight away. Similarly, it takes time to put up pictures of the child in the home and to adapt their environment to their tastes.

I remember that when I met my parents-in-law for the first time, they had a number of words, phrases and nicknames that were completely unfamiliar to me. For example, it would not be surprising to get a greetings card signed 'From me and Boot' from my in-laws. I still to this day do not know the story that makes my father-in-law's nickname Boot, but I have come to learn the story about other words. For example, they call instructions 'strollers', because my husband as a small boy could not pronounce 'instructions' and they thought his replacement was charming enough to continue. In their household, they also do a number of activities differently from my family. For example, they have a very flamboyant, extravagant Christmas with huge numbers of presents, most of them surprises. Whereas in my family, it was very low key and people could suggest a present they really wanted or ask someone else what they would like to be given.

These subtle but pervasive differences are between two white British households where the family members are of similar ages and levels of income. When we have friends to stay who come from more diverse backgrounds, more things diverge from their expectations. If you cross cultures or religions, then this also impacts. It is mind-blowing for me to try to imagine what it must feel like for a young person to move from a chaotic household with lots of siblings, and partners of their mother coming and going, in the midst of a council estate, into an adoptive home in the countryside where they are the only child. Yet children are placed in all kinds of family configurations, and matching cultural placements are not always available.

☀ Reflection: Building belonging

Think about the differences between your child's lifestyle in their family of origin and their lifestyle now. What has changed? Are there any things that seemed unfamiliar to them? To what extent were you able to find out about their typical daily routine or their normal environment before they came to you? Is there anything you could do to increase their sense of belonging (e.g., putting up their photos with the ones of your family you have on display or allowing them to customise their bedroom)? Does their life-story book, if they have one, include arriving at your home? If they don't have a life-story book, can you make one together, perhaps with the help of the child's social worker?

Sometimes, building belonging takes a long time and a lot of effort; sometimes, it happens almost by accident. 'Click' is the word used within the adoption research literature to describe the moment at which there is a sense of the child belonging within the family. There are sometimes the most incredible stories about something that connects the child with their new family, such as a liking for marmite and banana sandwiches or having a similar surgical scar to the adoptive or foster father. These little links can be incredibly powerful. However, they need to be told as a family story that uses the little links as examples of why you belong together.

Case examples: Click

I have been told a few amazing examples of 'clicks' during my professional life. One couple told me that they were trying for a baby when they moved to a new house. When they replaced the carpet, they found a book in the loft in which a young child had written 'Chris, age 5' and drawn a smiley face. They wished intensely for the kind of child who could have done that. Several years later, they decided to adopt a child, and when they were approved, they went to an event where video clips were played of children who were waiting for adoption. They were very attracted to a little boy with glasses and a mischievous grin, whose name was Chris. He moved in with them just after his fifth birthday.

Another couple told me how they had expressed interest in a girl with curly red hair they saw on a video clip. When the social worker had come round to visit to provide them more information about this child, she had asked them how they had obtained a photograph of the girl already. The photograph in question was one that the soon-to-be-adoptive-mother had dug out of an old photograph album showing images of her own mother during childhood.

These kinds of stories can be told to the child to illustrate how they belong in the family, but it can also be very mundane things that are used to make the same point. For example, being 'musical like Mummy', 'a natural gardener like Daddy', 'bossy like Mum', 'tall like Dad' or liking/hating Marmite or early mornings like other members of the family. Notice which parts of their appearance or mannerisms are similar to other members of the family. Talk about 'in our family we…' when explaining rules, ideas and beliefs about the world (e.g., 'In our family we try to be kind to others' or 'In our family we go to church on Sunday').

A related idea is whether you feel like you matter to anyone, and whether your views or well-being really matter to those making decisions about you. This appears to be very important in our sense of self and our mental health. The perception of 'anti-mattering', where you perceive that your views are deliberately ignored, contradicted or overridden, is associated with increased rates of depression and suicidal thinking. The qualities of care I described in Chapter 12 with the acronym PACE or PLACE should demonstrate to the child that they matter to you, in particular being curious about their perspective, and loving, accepting and empathic about their experiences and feelings.

CHAPTER 16

Stories

One of the other techniques that is really helpful in re-parenting children who have been exposed to chaos and trauma and abuse is to use stories. Lacher, Nichols, Nichols and May have written a book called *Connecting with Kids through Stories*,[1] which has some really good examples of how to do this and talks about 'claiming narratives'. Claiming narratives are a very powerful way of telling a child about what they deserved in their early life. So first of all you can talk about what was going on in your life at different points in the child's life. For example, 'We got the dog when you were two years old', 'We planted that tree around the time you were born' or 'We got married four years before you were born'. You might want to explain that 'We moved to this house when you were this old' or 'We went on this holiday when you were that old' or show them your photograph albums and relate the dates to events in their life.

Sharing your stories gives ownership of that background experience to that child. So if another child in the playground says 'I'm going to Disneyland in the summer', instead of that being completely foreign (as foreign as the tea-and-cake game in Chapter 6 is to someone who has only learnt the beer game), they can say 'My mum and dad went to Disneyland when I was two' or 'My mum and dad went to America the year before I was born'. Although it's not in the child's own repertoire, they will have a connection to more of the experiences within their new peer group if they have woven your stories into their own.

---

1   See Lacher *et al.* (2012).

The first thing about these narratives is that they interweave the child's story with your story, and that's really powerful, as they find connections and common ground that their securely attached peers would identify with. But the second and most important thing that happens with a claiming narrative is that you tell the child about the life that they deserve and the life you would have given them if you had been their caregiver from the start. You might want to tell the child this story in many parts and with increasing levels of detail if they are interested.

For example, you might tell them, 'I would have been so excited to have been pregnant with you! Your dad and I would have been so careful about what I ate all the way through the pregnancy and we would have started decorating the spare room and getting all the baby things. We would have been so excited to tell the news to Granny and Granddad and we would have gone out and bought baby shoes and little babygros and nappies.' You might want to actually take the child and show them those things in a baby shop or to buy some of those things to show the size of them and how small they are and how fragile a baby is. You might want to continue the story, explaining. 'If I was pregnant with you and nearly ready to give birth, I would have been this big [gesture with arms]. Come and curl up in front of me and let's see if Daddy can get his arms all the way round. You would have been inside my tummy, and I would have been so excited thinking you were going to arrive.'

Telling this story may be very difficult if you have adopted because of being infertile or after a difficult history of pregnancy, so you may wish to start with the newborn stages or the earliest that you can comfortably talk about with the child.

For example: 'When you arrived, you would have been so small and fragile that I would have been a little bit scared to hold you and I would have looked after you so carefully. Whenever you cried, I would have gone to see what it was. I would have been so anxious about whether you were breathing right, and I would have wanted you to sleep in my room. I would have been so careful about what I fed you, and I would have kept you really safe, and I would have made your room all nice and warm.' You can make the story as elaborate as you want, provided the child is interested, and you can focus on the aspects of care that the child has missed out on. It can be worth referring back to the brick-wall activity in Chapter 3 and thinking about which bricks are missing for your child, as these are the things you should detail in the claiming narrative.

This is a really clever technique, because it does not criticise the child's parent, who they might be loyal to, by saying everything that they did was wrong. It simply describes how you would have parented them given the opportunity.

You can emphasise areas in which their care was lacking to show what should have been provided. It is really important to demonstrate to children that they deserve to have good care, otherwise they will continue to associate the poor care they received with something innate about themselves, which in their mind means they deserve that level of care.

☼ Reflection: **Changing life**

At a very trivial level, you can imagine a small facet of what it must be like for children to move from one set of life experiences to another by imagining what it would be like if someone told you to brush your teeth before or after breakfast (whichever is the opposite to what you currently do). I know for me it would feel really uncomfortable to leave brushing my teeth as long as after breakfast, and to have to interact with people before I had brushed my teeth, but for some people the idea of having eaten breakfast and left your mouth dirty from breakfast would be equally uncomfortable.

Now imagine that you are a child and you are going from one household in which things are done in one way to another household in which many little detailed things are happening in a completely different way to the way you have always believed was the only way – the normal, right way of doing things. It would be very hard to adjust. I can only liken it to the experience of beginning to read a book, and learning all the characters' names, the plot, the setting, all of the beginnings of the story, and then starting chapter four and it having a different cast, a different setting and a different set of events happening. It would not make much sense if you were reading a book, and you would be waiting for something to connect the two experiences in order to feel that it was one coherent book. These young people have skipped from reading chapters one, two and three in their birth family, to chapters four and five in a foster home, maybe chapter six in a different foster home, and maybe only when they get to chapter seven are they in their permanent home. It must be very difficult to make sense of who these people are and the way the world works.

Using claiming narratives starts to interweave the story that came before and the way that you are doing things now. It also becomes a way of showing the child that you really want them to belong. You can project the story into the future by talking about what will happen when they start big school, when they finish school, when they start their job, when you are getting old, when you all go on holiday, when you reach Christmas and all the future points that give a child confidence that they will not have already moved on somewhere else by then.

The book by Lacher, Nichols, Nichols and May also has some useful techniques for using stories as metaphors for the experiences that children have been through, and we have found that very helpful with some young children. In this case example I have paraphrased an example of a story from the book that I have used.

Case example: The cat who was only a kitten herself

I was working with a family where the birth mother was very young and had learning difficulties, and kept returning to a violent alcoholic partner, despite spending time in a mother-and-baby unit and various refuges. Angel was about six by the time we used the story, and she remembered her mother as loving and could not understand why she had been 'rescued' into an adoptive family but her mother had not been.

The cat who was only a kitten herself

Once upon a time there was a kitten who lived in a barn on a farm. She met a big tough tomcat and got pregnant, but she was only a kitten herself, so she didn't know how to look after the new kittens that arrived when she gave birth. She tried to keep them clean, but the barn was very messy. She tried to feed them, but there wasn't much to eat. The tomcat would go out and try to hunt things for them to eat, and sometimes he got some food and sometimes he didn't. Sometimes he would drink water from the dirty puddles and it would make him feel a bit funny, and he would come back and hurt the cat who was only a kitten herself and scare the babies, but the cat felt safer when he was around, as the barn was kind of scary.

One day the farmer came into the barn and saw the cat who was only a kitten herself and her baby kittens. He could see that they looked hungry and scruffy and scared, so he took them into the farmhouse. In the farmhouse they got saucers of clean milk and some tasty food every morning and night. It was nice and warm and safe, but the cat who was only a kitten herself didn't know how to live in a farmhouse. She only knew how to live in a barn, so one day she ran off back to the tomcat in the barn. The farmer wanted to help her, but he couldn't keep her inside if she didn't want to stay, so all he could do was to keep looking after the baby kittens.

The baby kittens missed their mummy and wished she would stay in the house, but they didn't want to go back out to the scary cold barn again. They liked the other animals in the farmhouse, and the farmer and his wife were very kind to them, so they knew that they could have a good life there.

A colleague of mine, Dr Natalie Briant, was particularly creative at writing these kinds of stories with families, and the following examples are stories that we wrote together for particular children.

Case example: The jungle lion moves to the plain

I worked with a young girl whose mother had been very flamboyant at certain times and very self-neglectful in the low periods in between, during which she had let her hair get matted and would stay in bed for days at a time. The mother often had very unsafe partners around, some of whom had made sexual approaches to the children or been physically aggressive to them. Their household had been very chaotic, with a large sibling group and other people coming and going at all times. Netwe, the eight-year-old daughter from the family, really struggled with being removed from that household to a very quiet, calm foster placement in which she was the only child. She had also been very insistent about wanting to wear high heels, short skirts and make-up – I think, to mimic her mother's higher times.

You will remember that this is not an uncommon pattern. When you are used to the emotional volume being very high, it seems eerily quiet in these low-emotional-volume homes that children are placed in for adoption and fostering. But for the adoptive and foster parents, the child's emotional volume seems incredibly loud and out of place, and it is difficult for those two things to adjust to each other. In my experience, it takes really quite a long time for the child's arousal levels to come down to match the parents', a fact confirmed by research.[2] So we wanted to write a story to help the child make sense of this in metaphor form.

We wrote Netwe the following story:

The lion that moved from the jungle pack to the plains pack

In the jungle, pack life was very busy and noisy. There were a lot of cubs in the den, and there were lots of lions and other

---

2   Mary Dozier, an American professor of psychology, has been doing research where she swabs parents and children for cortisol and tracks what happens to cortisol patterns in different forms of placement. It is fascinating work and quite complex, but it is really confirming that arousal levels only begin to normalise when a child has been in a very predictable low-emotional-volume home for quite a long time, and that change is pretty slow. She has been developing interventions to maximise this.

animals around. The hyenas would come and want to be part of the pack, and they would laugh and have fun during the day but at night-time they were quite scary; they would snap their teeth and would often roll over onto the cubs and hurt them.

When the cub moved from the jungle pack to the plains pack, she found it very strange. She was the only cub with the two grown-up lions, and things seemed very quiet. There weren't any hyenas around and not so many other animals to play with. But she really wanted to try and fit in and belong and did not know how to. So she went out and looked at who the other animals seemed to like. Everybody liked the tiger, so the lion cub decided she wanted to be like the tiger. She went down to the river and found some brown mud and painted on stripes like a tiger to see if she could fit in better. But everybody teased her and laughed and pointed because of her stripes, so she went down to the watering hole and cried.

The elephant came down to the watering hole and said to her, 'Why are you crying?' She replied, 'Because I want everybody to like me, so I painted on stripes to be like the tiger, but nobody liked me.' The elephant was very wise and he said to her, 'The other animals like the tiger because she is kind and fair and honest and not because of her stripes. If you were kind and fair and honest, other animals would like you too. But it will take some time.' He gently squirted some water on her so that she could wash off the muddy remains of her stripes. When she followed the elephant's advice, the lion learnt to make friends with the other animals that lived on the plains and began to enjoy life living in the quiet plains pack. Having two adult lions all to herself meant there was always food to eat and plenty of room in the den, which always felt safe. That let her grow up big and strong.

The story acts as a metaphor for the child's experience and can be evolved according to the child's response to it. For example, if Netwe had said 'The hyenas used to squash the cubs so they couldn't breathe', that could be built into the story (and might be a really helpful disclosure about her past experience). Likewise if she said 'The hyenas didn't snap their teeth or roll onto the cubs, they just got drunk and done sex with the mummy lion all the time', then the story should be corrected (and again, you have potentially learnt something more about the child's history).

The stories you write and tell can also reflect different aspects of the child's experience. This can be their current or future experience as well as metaphors for their past trauma. So, for example, Natalie wrote a story about a car that was stuck in reverse for a boy who was oppositional. The story gave empathy for the pattern he had learnt but also showed how he could benefit from sometimes choosing to do as he was told. Other stories can be written to prepare for a successful future, whether this is in terms of explaining what happens when we go on holiday or imagining being a grown-up and still within the family.

ACTIVITY: TELLING STORIES

Think about the messages you would like to convey to your child. Try to write a story to tell your child that conveys these messages. The easiest place to start is with a 'claiming narrative' that interweaves their milestones with events in your life and tells the child how you would have cared for them if you'd been given the opportunity. See if you can write a short story about this to tell to your child.

You will need to find the right opportunity to tell the story. Perhaps it can be at bedtime or when the child is sitting on your knee on the sofa, is wrapped up snug in a blanket or is stuck in the back of the car for a long journey. Tell a fairly short, simple story, and allow the child to ask for expansion if they want (or you can tell more if they seem interested). If the child does not seem interested, or is physically active or not making eye contact, keep telling the story. Sometimes the content of the story will raise the child's physiological arousal and mean they need to fidget or be active, but in my experience, they will still be listening! It is worth revisiting the story several times, and seeing the child's reaction. Give empathy if they appear to be trying to distract from or avoid the story. If the child shows interest, you might end up expanding on it and retelling it many times, and finding parts of the story brought up in conversation later down the line. This shows the child is connecting the story to their internal narrative about their life.

CHAPTER 17

Time Holes and Triggers

The concept of 'time holes' is a really useful idea that was first described by Angela Hobday, a clinical psychologist with a lot of personal and professional experience of adoption and fostering. She talks about a time hole being a useful image when a young person's reaction is disproportionate to what is going on in the present. For example, if you ask a child to turn off the television and that leads to a rage where they are attacking you, destroying their toys, pulling out their hair or screaming and sobbing in a corner, that would be disproportionate to the present trigger and would almost always relate to something in the past. Angela Hobday uses the image of falling through a time hole to describe how that response to the situation comes from the past. I have illustrated this in Doodle 23.

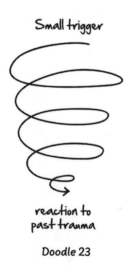

Doodle 23

Case example: Ugh, you're disgusting!

I worked with a foster family where a boy called Mike had been with them for four years. He'd had a very neglectful early background and he'd been allowed to get very dirty and had often been sent to nursery with a full nappy and stained clothing. Because he was dirty and smelly, other children had come to regard him as very unattractive to play with, so he had been very left out and scapegoated. The staff at nursery had often tried to clean his clothes and change him, to make life nicer for him, but this was insufficient to keep him in a presentable state.

When I worked with the foster family, they told me that Mike was having rages that had no apparent trigger. I asked them to tell me about the last time that Mike had gone into a rage. They told me, 'It was a really lovely day in which several friends of the family had come over with their children and everybody was eating burgers. It should have been a really lovely time but Mike went off in a rage and ruined it.' I asked them to unpick that for me and tell me exactly what was going on. They told me that Mike had bitten into his burger and a splodge of ketchup had fallen onto the table. As many of us might do in the privacy of our own homes, Mike had used the burger to scoop up the ketchup that had dropped out and had carried on eating. Someone else at the table had said 'Ugh, that's disgusting' and pointed their fingers at Mike. That had been the trigger for an extreme rage in which he had knocked everything off the surfaces in the dining room and had gone up to his bedroom and started smashing the toys that they had given him for his birthday.

It was really clear to see, with the idea of time holes, that being pointed at and described as disgusting was a very powerful trigger for Mike to feel what he felt when he was the little boy who was neglected and smelly and dirty and nobody wanted to play with him. He felt like he did not deserve a good life, so he had destroyed all the trappings of the good life he had now been given, by knocking everything off the surfaces to make a mess and destroying all the toys that he did not think he deserved. This is an incredibly powerful reaction to something, which really makes sense when you understand the history but makes no sense with only the information available in the here and now.

Angela Hobday talked about a time when she was handing out packets of crisps from a multipack. I am sure you can picture the scene of different people in the household asking for ready salted, or salt and vinegar, or cheese and onion or smoky bacon flavour, and she was throwing the packets of crisps to people. She said that when she threw a packet of crisps for one of her daughters, she cowered. Angela Hobday said that she suddenly realised she had learnt something new about her daughter: that at some point in her history, before she had been in their family, someone had thrown things at her in a way that could have hurt her.

Time holes are a really powerful concept, and they are a really great opportunity for empathy. If you can help the child to connect the experiences that led to the feelings that led to the behaviour, you can help them understand why they feel and behave the way that they do. This allows them to view themselves in a different way. Instead of becoming a reinforcement of shame that they are a bad kid and did something with no reason, it becomes part of their increasing ability to apply that frontal-lobe thinking that connects cause and effect and makes life into a coherent narrative in which you can change how you think about things or how you behave, in order to get different experiences and to have better experiences in future.

It is also useful to think about sensory triggers. We often associate memories with smells or sounds, for example. Many people have strong associations with particular songs, or the smell of honeysuckle, or fish and chips, or a cake baking in the oven. Sometimes those memories are pleasant, like a first date, or cooking with a parent as a young child, or the smell of someone's home or perfume that you associate with comfort and safety. But sometimes those memories are of less pleasant memories, of times that something bad happened or of someone that was harmful to you, and it can be this that you are reminded of when you meet similar sensory experiences again.

I have a small example, from my first job in psychology. My office was on the third floor of an old building, and there was a grand old staircase that wound around the lift, that I would walk up and down each day. One day I was walking down the stairs to get to the canteen for lunch. I was talking to a colleague when I missed my footing. Thankfully I only fell down about eight steps, because there was a quarter-landing where the stairs changed direction, but it gave me quite a fright. I also cut my calf quite badly on the metal trim on the edge of the step. My first thought was embarrassment. I tried to pick myself up and pretend it had never happened, but by the bottom of the stairs I was going into shock and kind medical colleagues sat me down with my head low until I felt less faint, then bandaged my leg and took me home. I was fine and had no lasting ill effects from the injury. However, it made me a lot more wary when walking down stairs. Even 25 years later, that feeling of dread and the tightness in my stomach is something I still feel when going down long straight escalators on the underground. I think I probably had the thought 'That could have killed me if there hadn't been a turn in the stairs' as I got up from my fall. So the long straight descent of an escalator and the metal teeth that edge each step feel dangerous to me. It is a salient reminder that the body holds on to survival learning for a long time, even where this isn't in our conscious awareness. If someone like me, who has had a very safe life and all the benefits of loving relationships and the insights of psychology, can't stop my stomach lurching when I get on an escalator, I can understand that young people who have experienced many threats and trau- matic experiences might have multiple triggers that can set their body into fight-or-flight mode without their conscious awareness understanding why.

The human brain particularly hangs on to any association with threat, to maximise our future chances of survival – and we learn from when others show fear in reaction to things. That is why so many people are wary of snakes or spiders or heights. For people who have been in war zones, the sounds of explosions and the smell of gunpowder or things burning can bring back traumatic memories. Other people are triggered by the sight or smell of hospitals, or depictions of violence or abuse on TV or in the media. But we also learn from more mundane or personal experiences to associate feelings of comfort and safety or discomfort and wariness with various situations or sensations. For example, we learn not to eat too much of things that can make us sick, to touch things that are hot or to play with electricity because of the consequences we associate with them. This learning can also apply to how we interact with people; we learn the signs in their posture, facial expression or tone of voice that indicate someone is in a bad mood, so that we can avoid making them angry. Children can be incredibly sensitive to these changes in tone, and will often report being 'shouted at' if they hear even the smallest shift towards a cross voice. This sensitivity to small cues becomes very important to survival if you are a small child in a chaotic or unsafe environment or have to deal with adults who can be harmful towards you.

Early trauma may be remembered in terms of bodily sensations, and a reminder of those sensations can suddenly take the child back to the trauma. At those times, the child may be cut off from their ability to look at their experiences verbally or cognitively and may be immersed in debilitating fear or shame. Painful and frightening memories may have been pushed aside but still disturb the child and their relationships. Reminders of trauma could be in the form of smells, sounds, textures, tastes, tone or pitch of voice or any other memory. I have had children talk about how they associate the toast popping out the toaster with the domestic violence incident that led to their father's arrest and their removal into Care. I have worked with a child who was struck with fear whenever they heard the sound of someone stirring their tea, as their sadistic grandfather was the only person in their household to take sugar. I have met children who associate the texture of raw egg white with sexual abuse. It is fairly common for a more fearful response to be triggered in children by people of a certain age and one particular gender or by particular characteristics – glasses, a deep voice, the smell of a particular perfume or overweight women.

It is also really common for children to learn to play out a different pattern with different members of the family, depending on the roles that particular individuals took with the child in their past experience, and how the child has associated these past experiences with the people currently involved in their life. So, for example, they might be really difficult and oppositional with their adoptive mother and act in ways that make her feel inadequate or angry, but they might be playful and compliant with their adoptive father. This can make it really tricky for the other adults to empathise with how the primary carer is feeling, as they only see much more positive patterns from the child. This can put strain on relationships, where one person feels blamed or inadequate because the child is more difficult with them or feels that the other adult doesn't understand. It may also be that one adult falls in love with the child, whilst the other doesn't have the same feelings straight away. Or it might be that one person is somehow repulsed by something the child does, whether that is the sudden exposure to bodily fluids and mess that young children bring or the discomfort of a sexual undertone to the way a child behaves.

When these 'splits' happen, it is really important to talk about your different experiences and to consider where the different patterns originate and what echoes they have in your own life. Certain things are much more loaded if you have had certain experiences yourself. For example, I have met several adoptive and foster carers who have been really bothered about whether or not a child could have been sexually abused, and have found it incredibly hard to deal with any hint of sexualised behaviour, because of experiences in their own lives. Similarly, some carers find themselves getting really angry with a child who is rude or ungrateful or always wants the last word if these were things that were against the rules in their own childhood, whilst their partner might not be bothered at all. Or there might be things that the child does that remind you of yourself or someone else in the family that change how you interact with them because of that past template. I've seen children treated with less sympathy because they remind a parent of themselves, but I've also seen children who remind carers of a sibling or parent that they had a difficult relationship with. These situations are really worth talking about with someone from outside the family. In psychology, the concepts of 'transference' and 'countertransference' refer to bringing past relationships into new ones and how that can make you react in a way that shows feelings that are displaced in time or from one person to another.

Another situation that can be very destructive within a placement is if a child makes allegations against someone within the family. It is very difficult to balance trusting the child and taking seriously their allegations whilst also protecting someone that you know and care about. Even where allegations are clearly false and can be rapidly dismissed by the professional network, it can feel like a huge betrayal and be very hard to have continued empathy for the child. However, it is worth bearing in mind that a lot of children who have experienced abuse have tried to make disclosures in the past and not been heard or believed. Thus, when their relationships and environment have changed, it makes sense that they would want to know if they would be believed within the new situation. This would help them to check whether their past experience was normal and acceptable, but also make them feel safer. I described one example of this in Chapter 11, where the child had exaggerated an incident in which they were smacked, having already told a somewhat skewed tale about being deprived. Another example occurred in my therapy work.

Case example: Guilty or not guilty?

I worked with a 12-year-old called Saranya who had some developmental delay. She had been removed from her family of origin after chronic neglect. The foster carers told me that they felt she 'carried a heavy burden' and had never talked about her experiences in the birth family. Because her spoken language was not very good, I offered some play-based sessions. She soon established a pattern of setting up a court in the playroom, with various cuddly toys playing the victim, the perpetrator and the judge. Over many sessions, she explored whether the victim's disclosure being believed or disbelieved, the perpetrator denying or accepting the charge (and whether or not he said sorry) and the judge finding the defendant guilty or not guilty had an impact on whether or not the event really happened and how the victim felt about it. When she established that I believed that the victim was the only person who really knew what happened, and that the truth was the truth regardless of what the perpetrator or judge said, she was able to begin to disclose sexual abuse from her birth father. It seemed he had confused her with repeated denials that this had happened, an apology that he said undid everything that came before it and the persuasive idea that no one would believe her if she disclosed but he denied it. This was also reinforced by cultural beliefs within her Jehovah's Witness community, where speaking or thinking badly of anyone within the church was considered to be as bad as anything they had done. Sadly, but not atypically in my experience, she was not able to make the disclosures against her father clearly enough in a police interview set up for achieving best evidence, and no charges were ever pressed for her to test what the real result would have been in court.

CHAPTER 18

Patterns That Suck Us In

We all have certain patterns that we repeat over and over again because they are learnt ways to behave in particular situations. Some of these are helpful patterns, like how to make the right body movements to swim, cycle or drive the car, or how to comfort a crying baby. However, sometimes we repeat patterns that are less helpful. We end up feeling frustrated and angry, but we can't seem to help ourselves. For example, some people have had experiences of being criticised and made to feel small by others who are trying to make themselves feel clever or powerful. They might then respond in a much stronger way to perceived criticism, either by feeling small and shamed or by trying to assert that they are powerful or superior. They might continue to do this even if the results are unhelpful, for example in response to feedback from a superior in the workplace. In the language of Dr Anthony Ryle, who developed a form of therapy to work with people with very entrenched problems in relating to others, these patterns have become 'traps'.[1] For example, we might get a fixed idea about a 'false choice', where we think that we have to always be at one extreme of a particular concept. So I might think that 'Either I give in and please others but feel taken advantage of or I refuse and everybody hates me' or 'Either I am critical and superior or I feel criticised and worthless'. These roles might be learnt from how we interact with a parent, where one

---

[1] His Cognitive Analytic Therapy is particularly helpful for people with personality disorder, which I view as 'attachment disorder grown up' in that it is a pattern of relating to others developed through the long-term impact of chronic trauma, abuse and neglect.

side of the choice is how the parent behaved and the other how the child behaved.

I find it useful to think about the reciprocal roles that take place between a parent and a child. These are patterns where each side is a response to the other and reinforces the other (see Doodle 24). An example is a child who has learnt that most of the time they are ignored and have to be self-sufficient (but feel non-existent as a result): the child makes no demands on the parent and so the parent provides nothing for the child, but the child has learned to make no demands because the parent is not available to make demands of and is not providing any input. Similarly, the child may learn to be very provocative and demanding so that this definitely gets a response, but the response may be very negative and punitive because the parent is not able to be child-centred and simply sees the child as being naughty.

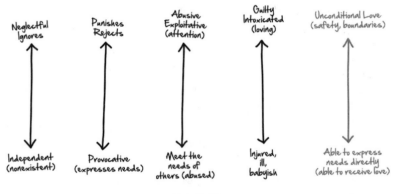

Doodle 24

A child may learn to take up a role that gets some positive feedback, whether by meeting the adult's needs (including by taking care of them, or colluding with sexual abuse) or creating guilt or sympathy by being ill, injured or babyish. The child may not have learned the pattern most prevalent in families where secure attachment is the norm, whereby they are able to express needs directly and receive unconditional love and support. So when they experience someone being loving, they wonder which of their established patterns it fits into – is the adult wanting something in return or do they feel guilty or sorry for me? If this unfamiliar pattern feels too threatening, they might do something to return to their familiar patterns by behaving in a way that is provocative and invites punishment or by ignoring and rejecting the approach in the way their neglectful parent would. As you can see from this example, the child learns the role that they experience in return, as well as the means to trigger each response from their parent. This means the child learns the behaviours on both sides of each arrow in the doodle.

You will remember from earlier chapters how important it is to recognise the underlying need and not to just take the expressed need at face value. If a child has learnt to be overly self-sufficient and mature, then you could unwittingly reinforce this by following their messages and thus letting them continue to be more autonomous than the norm for their age and reducing the amount of nurture you would normally offer. It is therefore important to ensure that you also meet the unexpressed need to provide the nurture, reassurance and affection that might be unfamiliar or uncomfortable for the child. Or the child might express a high level of anxiety, require constant adult attention and find it impossible to do anything autonomously, as if the idea is terrifying. Again, if you just meet the expressed need, you reinforce the pattern of dependence and an anxious ambivalent relationship pattern, so it is important to meet the unexpressed need and encourage some independence and exploration even if the child resists this. No matter what pattern the child tries to pull you into, it is important that you are thoughtful about whether this is helpful for them for you to play along with or not, and whether it addresses the underlying need that they have. It is important to meet the child's unexpressed underlying needs and to demonstrate that a different pattern is possible.

Case example: Who has the biggest teeth?

I worked with a care leaver called Jamila who had been through a large number of different placements. She had a very chaotic lifestyle, with lots of conflict in her social group, and was 'couch surfing' from one address to another with no permanent accommodation of her own. Jamila had a string of relationships with males involved in crime and violence, many of whom treated her very badly. She was often the victim of domestic violence and assaults, and twice of rape. She had also claimed to be pregnant several times, with various stories about lost pregnancies, although only one miscarriage was recorded in her medical notes.

When I worked with Jamila, I was somewhat overwhelmed by the level of chaos in her life, but it gradually began to form some patterns. One of these was that she was often attracted to a man she perceived as being fierce enough to defend her from the previous man once they had fallen out. We talked about how in her world the ideal man was a wolf who had big sharp teeth to fend off danger from others, but the risk was that he would turn his teeth on her. She had learnt to mitigate this risk by claiming to be pregnant.

As we worked together, I was able to identify that this pattern had been formed early in her life. There had been a number of violent and sexually abusive men around during her childhood, and she had learnt that she could trade sex for protection from the physical aggression that felt like a constant risk. Whenever anyone was kind to her (even a parent figure), she assumed that they were only attracted to her as a potential sexual partner, and her sexualised response had made a lot of carers very uncomfortable and contributed to her high rate of placement breakdown. When I engaged in therapy with her, we explicitly talked about the nature of this new relationship for her and how I was going to act as a safe, non-sexual, non-threatening person to prove that such a relationship existed. She found it very hard to fit that into her template of relationship patterns. At times she appeared to try to provoke me into rejecting her by being insulting or refusing to do the work we had agreed. I came away from sessions feeling a whole range of emotions including sympathy, guilt, frustration and anger. The latter was certainly not typical of my feelings towards a vulnerable young woman but was something she was able to provoke even in someone as placid as me, due to her recurrent experiences of relating to people who were aggressive.

Just as I have related in my own experience above, a lot of non-birth-parent carers tell me that they sometimes feel very angry or uncomfortable with the child and don't know where these feelings came from. They are often highly self-critical about these feelings (e.g., crying and telling me that they didn't adopt a child to yell at him or have thoughts of shaking or hitting him). This is the hallmark of being sucked into someone else's patterns. You end up enacting the opposite pole of the reciprocal role brought from the child's history,[2] that is, you feel drawn to react in the way that the child is expecting you to react, which is based on their family of origin. This is very uncomfortable because such abusive ways of interacting are not in our own repertoire.

In those situations, I find it useful to 'name the game and change the game'. That is, to say something like: 'I think you are trying to make me feel angry with you. Let's go and do something different.' However, it can be really difficult to recognise the patterns before you are completely sucked into playing them out. We can also fall into patterns that do come from our own repertoire, but we really don't want to re-enact, and had hoped we wouldn't ever use – like replaying the kind of critical or punitive parenting that we experienced. Both of these situations are really worth talking to someone outside the family about, and are familiar areas to work on for psychologists and psychotherapists. But just recognising there is a pattern you are falling into is the most important first step.

I find the poem 'An autobiography in five short chapters' by Portia Nelson helpful in this regard. In the first verse, she walks down a road and falls into a hole, which is scary and takes a long time to get out of. In the next verse, she walks down the road and falls into the hole, which is familiar and easier to get out of. In the

---

2   Non-birth parents can feel drawn to react how the child is expecting them to react. See Archer and Gordon (2006).

third verse, she walks down the road, sees the hole coming but falls in it anyway but is able to get out quickly. In the fourth verse, she walks down the road, sees the hole and is able to walk around it. In the fifth verse, she walks down a different road. This poem reminds us that if we hit a challenge that we can't overcome immediately, it might take some time to tackle. We first need to recognise being in it and practise getting out of it quickly before we can learn to see it coming and avoid it altogether.

ACTIVITY: MAPPING OUT PATTERNS

You may find that your child repeats and repeats certain patterns, despite them not leading to a successful outcome. You may be able to map out their patterns with the reciprocal role pairs like I have illustrated in Doodle 24. If you are able to recognise patterns whilst they are playing out, this would be a good time to use empathy to link their past experiences and what they have learnt to the current problems. It can also be an opportunity to use a story to highlight the pattern and make it safe to talk about, so that you can point out when it is happening and help the child to see it coming.

It may be that when you map out the patterns, you find you are unwittingly being drawn into them. This is a very good thing to know! I remember when I first started mapping some of my therapy relationships in my supervision and realised there were patterns that had sucked me in. I was unwittingly playing out roles I was uncomfortable with and reinforcing unhealthy patterns for the other person. That was quite a revelation, but it was really helpful to learn, as it meant I could be aware of the processes and reflect them to the person I was working with. So, don't be ashamed. Simply work out how you are going to react differently in future and start to actively tackle the problem – and if it is too hard to do so alone, get some support to help you.

USING YOUR SUPPORT NETWORK

The other important thing to do is to recognise when you need outside help. I find that a lot of adoptive and foster parents feel like they have had to prove themselves so much that they think they should not show signs of weakness and need to be the perfect parent who is able to tackle every eventuality on their own. However, it is actually a strength to recognise when you need some support, and much preferable to saying 'It's fine, it's fine, it's fine' until you have to say 'It's broken beyond repair' when it comes to professionals' understanding of how the placement is going. We would much rather meet a caregiver who is able to identify difficulties early in the process so that we can support them to tackle the issues than one who waits until they are overwhelming and risks the placement breaking down. If you think back to the tug-of-war illustrations in Doodles 13–15, it is important to recognise when you are being pulled out of your secure base or when you have extra life stresses going on that don't relate to the child and might reduce your resources (e.g., problems with your relationship, health, employment, finances, mental health, the additional needs of dependants, etc.). Hopefully, some professional support or personal therapy can help you to stay in the secure pattern yourself and feel well informed and understood when it comes to the needs of your child.

It is also useful to remember that hearing about a child's traumatic experiences can cause you what is known as secondary trauma. If you care about a child and hear about the awful things that they have been through, and can picture scenes of abuse or violence, then this is naturally going to be upsetting and can stay with you for a long time. Kate Cairns has written a lot about the impact of secondary trauma and believes it is one of the hardest aspects to being a non-birth-parent carer. I find it somewhat ironic that the people we most want to step forward as adoptive and foster parents are those who can really hold the child in mind and offer them sincere empathy, but it is these very qualities that make you susceptible to being traumatised by the stories the child brings from their past experiences. As a therapist, I have many support networks in place to help me to deal with those images and feelings, but in your personal life they can really cause distress that you don't have a means to process. Again, if talking to your personal and professional support network is not sufficient, I would really recommend seeking out some personal therapy in this situation.

It might also be that you want to share information about the attachment difficulties your child is experiencing with other members of the family, your friends, the child's school or nursery, or other sections of your network. They might benefit from a better understanding of attachment and trauma too, and it might help them to respond in a more sympathetic way to some of the challenges they are experiencing with the child. Provided you aren't telling all the child's intimate details to those that don't need to know about them, this is entirely appropriate and will mean that you can all support each other and work in a consistent way so that the child gains maximum benefit. You might like to lend them this book!

There are also a range of professionals who might be able to help you. Social workers (and various other social care or agency staff like family support workers or link workers) can provide advice and support for yourselves or the child. There will also be input from teachers and, depending on the child's needs, from health professionals like GPs or paediatricians. Where the issues are with mental health (which may show through behaviour, emotions or relationships), or with the child's development, there are a whole range of mental health professionals and therapists that you might come into contact with, including clinical psychologists like me. Where things are very complicated or stuck, there can end up being a whole team around the child, trying to work together in different ways to help.

If a child is having difficulties with their mental health, sending the child to therapy might seem to be the obvious answer, as that is portrayed as the (almost magical) way to solve all mental health issues. However, in reality the most important relationship is between the child and their primary caregiver. It might surprise you to know that you probably spend more time with your child in a weekend than a therapist will spend with them in six months. I also believe that where the damage has been done in the context of caregiving relationships, the repair predominantly needs to be done within caregiving relationships. For these reasons, my role will most often be to support the parent or carer rather than working directly with the child. Psychologists often assess children to help understand their needs better, and some may do 'dyadic' work (with parent and child together, like the Dan Hughes model of therapy that is so helpful when attachment relationships are blocked, or the specialist play-based way of working called Theraplay), but it is only with older children who are willing and able to talk about their issues that the evidence for direct therapeutic work is strong enough to make that the primary intervention. Whilst there may be individual reasons that these types of therapy are recommended, the evidence for play therapy or other non-directive sessions for children who have experienced trauma or attachment issues is quite limited and suggests that it works more as a break for parents, teachers, siblings and peers than as a means to create change within the child. Usually change happens across a whole family system, and is gradual and cumulative. If you are able to understand the child's needs and how they relate to their early experience, and to respond to the child with empathy, then you will be making those changes day after day. Even the simple everyday actions of making regular meals, providing clean clothes and having a comfortable home will change the child's world. Giving your attention to the child and caring how they feel, trying to help them and be kind to them, day in day out, are the best ingredients to help your child along the journey towards trusting others and believing in themselves.

CHAPTER 19

Heroes

As an end note, I'd like to think about what makes a hero. It is an activity that I get people to think about in my groups fairly often. I ask participants to think of someone from history or the present, reality or fiction, who has qualities that they admire. This might be a character from a book, film or game, a sportsperson, a politician or activist, a community leader, a member of their family or any other character or individual. I then ask them to talk about what they admire about that person and what qualities helped them to stand out.

I've heard people talk about their parents or grandparents struggling in difficult circumstances, perhaps as a single parent or someone experiencing prejudice from others. Or people in their network who have coped with adversity, like a disability or sudden misfortune. I've heard about people that put themselves at risk to take up a cause, like those who hid Jews from the Nazis. I've heard about community activists and politicians, like Aneurin Bevan forming the NHS or those who fought for voting rights for women or the end of slavery. Some people talk about individuals who have been exceptional at their sport or are talented actors or singers, but often it is the extra actions people take beyond their primary role that lead to admiration, like Dolly Parton's contribution to causes including vaccine research and regeneration of an impoverished neighbourhood. When people talk about fictional superheroes it is often the choice they have made to use their gifts to help others, or stories where they have had to make personal sacrifice, that cause people to admire them, rather than the special gifts that they have been given.

Reflection: Heroes

Have a think about your own personal heroes. What qualities do they possess? What makes them stand out from the norm? What do you admire about them?

In the group, when we combine all our responses to these questions, regardless of who people have chosen as heroes, we normally end up with a spider diagram like Doodle 25. We see that people admire qualities like being tenacious, putting in effort, being willing to speak up for others or step up to the block, and sticking with tricky challenges.

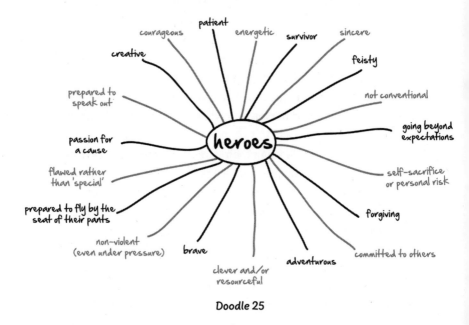

Doodle 25

Next, I ask people to consider which of these qualities they can identify in themselves and/or their child. I hope you will be able to recognise quite a few. Foster and adoptive parents are often amazingly selfless, resilient, persistent, compassionate people who advocate for the needs of their children. It takes an amazing person to choose to care for a child who has experienced abuse and neglect, and to stand by them when their behaviour is challenging, but the majority of parents I have worked with are too humble to acknowledge this.

I previously mentioned an animation by Hayao Miyazaki. Well, one of the things that makes me love his work is his belief that 'a hero is an ordinary person who rises to a challenge'. I strongly agree with that definition, and on that basis, I've met a lot of heroes in my groups and clinics!

The Impact of Poor Early Care

Early care begins from before the child is even born. Exposure to violence, drugs or alcohol during pregnancy has a lasting impact on the unborn baby. Fight or flight neurochemicals can travel in the bloodstream from the mother to the foetus, priming them for an unsafe world. A sensitive parent who is empathic to the needs of their unborn child is less likely to expose them to such risks, and will often begin to build the relationship with their child through movement, touch, talking and singing. They often also begin to imagine their baby's thoughts and feelings, imbuing their movements with meaning and making guesses about the child's personality. From birth that process increases into a complex interplay between parent and child, in which the child begins to make sense of their sensory experiences and to learn about themselves in the mirror of their parents' reactions to them.

The type of attachment relationship formed between a parent and their infant has a powerful influence on the potential health, social and economic opportunities of that child throughout their lifetime. This is particularly remarkable given that the template for a child's attachment relationship style is largely determined before the age of two. Attachment style has an impact on a huge variety of psychosocial outcomes, including academic achievements, marital satisfaction, likelihood of criminal involvement, mental health and quality of relationship with their own children (Sainsbury Centre for Mental Health, 2009). Correlations are also evidenced between childhood trauma and the incidence of chronic diseases in adulthood, and the impact of these diseases on functioning and healthcare uptake (Feeney, 2000; Raque-Bogdan *et al.*, 2011). For example, attachment style is shown to influence health outcomes in childhood infections and asthma, cancer and diabetes (Bazzazian and Besharat, 2012; Cicero *et al.*, 2009; Ciechanowski *et al.*, 2004; Mäntymaa *et al.*, 2003; Tacon, 2003; Tacon, Caldera and Bell, 2001). The Adverse Childhood Experiences study (Felitti *et al.*, 1998) showed that the impact of childhood adversity is cumulative and long-lasting. The CDC has a summary of the numerous findings on its website.[1]

There is complex interplay between a baby's experiences and their neurological development, with optimal development being more likely where a parent is physically and psychologically available, attuned to the infant's needs and able to hold that child in mind. It is sensitive interaction with the caregiver that teaches a child to regulate their physiological arousal level, to recognise their emotions and to 'mentalise' or understand the nature of minds (Meins *et al.*, 1998). Early attachment experiences have been shown to influence brain development, with early exposure to trauma and a lack of nurture leading to a state of heightened physiological arousal and differences in cortisol production (Bruce *et al.*, 2009; Gunnar and Vazquez, 2001). This increased readiness for fight or flight can show in anxious or aggressive behaviour, and may mean the child is less effective at empathy, emotional regulation and executive functions like planning and anticipating the effect of behaviour. This can lead to problems in the family and/or school (which may be conceptualised as internal to the child, e.g., ADHD) and lead to referrals to educational support services and CAMHS. Early life stress confers risk for later psychopathology such as anxiety, depression, post-traumatic stress, substance use and psychosis (Mueller *et al.*, 2010). Maltreatment also appears to increase the probability of a neurodevelopmental condition (Dinkler *et al.*, 2017).

Maternal/parenting factors are a huge influence on the attachment style of the infant, with depression, stress and social or partner support being particularly influential (Atkinson *et al.*, 2000; Halligan,

---

1   See www.cdc.gov/violenceprevention/aces/index.html

2007). Interventions which help mothers to improve their mental health, reduce stress and increase mentalisation and self-compassion have been shown to improve the attachment and outcomes for their infants (Cree, 2010; Neff and McGehee, 2010). Such early interventions have been shown to be highly cost effective and to make lasting changes for the life outcomes of the next generation (Sainsbury Centre for Mental Health, 2009).

When attachment relationships or the early environment are so dysfunctional that the child is removed into Care, this picture of increased risks of negative outcomes is exaggerated further still. Whilst the majority of children in Care go on to happy and productive lives, statistically Care leavers are 50 times more likely to go to prison, 88 times more likely to be involved in drug use and 60 times more likely to be homeless than those who have never been in Care (Barnardo's *et al.*, 2000). This means that we are not yet managing to address all the needs of children in the Care system, as their pre-Care experiences are still making them vulnerable to risks in adulthood; and when children are moved frequently from one placement to another, their experiences in Care can compound this.

We know that 75 per cent of children in Care have significant mental health needs, with over 50 per cent having a diagnosable mental health condition (Tarren-Sweeney, 2010). The later a child is removed into Care, the more maltreatment they have experienced and the more placements they pass through in Care, the higher the risk to their mental health, personal relationships and outcomes in adult life. Placement breakdowns are more common for teenagers with mental health problems that are associated with the young people's histories of sexual abuse, neglect and exposure to domestic violence. It seems that serious or worsening mental health problems might be a 'red flag' indicating when additional support is required. Yet access to skilled mental health support, especially for complex needs that cannot be resolved through short-term interventions intended to target mild presentations of depression and anxiety, is harder to access than ever before.

With the right support, the vast majority of children go on to happy and productive lives. Finding a permanent or long-term home with caregivers who can offer a secure attachment is a key part of that. Adoption has been shown to be the most powerful intervention ever studied (van IJzendoorn and Juffer, 2005), with permanent placement in a new loving home giving the children improved outcomes on every measure – higher IQ and reduced mental health and behavioural needs. The earlier they reach that permanent home the better the outcomes are. We see this in the outcomes for adoption, when children are typically removed in the first two years of life and placed in their new family at an average age of three. More than 96 per cent of children who are adopted remain successfully in their new family until adulthood (Selwyn, Wijedasa and Meakings, 2014). However, there are not enough adoptive parents to place many children who could be adopted, so many children (particularly those in sibling groups, with disabilities or from ethnic minorities) end up staying in the Care system. Some of those find wonderful foster placements, but there is also a shortage of suitable foster carers, so matching decisions are often influenced by supply and demand more than being able to pick the right carers to match a child's needs. I strongly believe that older children also deserve to have permanent homes and secure attachment relationships. Part of that should be a shift in government policy to improve the status and pay of foster carers, so that we can recruit more foster parents, as well as promoting adoption and reaching out to a wider pool of potential adopters. My research shows that finding adoptive parents who are motivated to make a difference for a child that really needs them might attract a different group of people to those motivated to fill a gap within their family caused by not being able to have a child biologically. Likewise, there is room to encourage a greater cohort of therapeutic foster parents who are supported by a professional network to meet the needs of children with more complex needs.

A lot of work is being done to try to improve systems and services to ensure that children receive help earlier (e.g., the Independent Care Review, 2022), but unfortunately they have not focused on the need for more specialist mental health input for this population. I passionately believe that identifying mental health needs and providing timely access to psychological support is critical in giving every child the best chance in life to recover from any Adverse Childhood Experiences or maltreatment. For that reason, I have made it my mission to develop tools to identify, track and support the mental health needs of vulnerable children for both organisations/professionals and parents. My tools have not only been shown to help children to make more progress, but they can also be used to match children to appropriate placements, helping a greater number of children to find a permanent home within a family. You can read more about this work at BERRI.org.uk and perhaps help to spread the word and make services better for children who have had a tough start in life.

APPENDIX REFERENCES

Atkinson, L., Paglia, A., Coolbear, J., Niccols, A., Parker, K. and Guger., S. (2000) 'Attachment security: A meta-analysis of maternal mental health correlates.' *Clinical Psychology Review 20*, 8, 1019–1040.

Barnardo's, Child Poverty Action Group, Children in Wales, The Children's Society, NSPCC and SCF (2000) *Wales' Children, Our Future – A Manifesto.*

Bazzazian, S. and Besharat, M. (2012) 'An explanatory model of adjustment to type I diabetes based on attachment, coping, and self-regulation theories.' *Psychology, Health & Medicine 17*, 1, 47–58.

Bruce, J., Fisher, P.A., Pears, K.C. and Levine, S. (2009) 'Morning cortisol levels in preschool-aged foster children: Differential effects of maltreatment type.' *Developmental Psychobiology 51*, 1, 14–23.

Cicero, V., Lo Coco, G., Gullo, S. and Lo Verso, G. (2009) 'The role of attachment dimensions and perceived social support in predicting adjustment to cancer.' *Psycho-Oncology 18*, 10, 1045–1052.

Ciechanowski, P., Russo, J., Katon, W., Von Korff, M., *et al.* (2004) 'Influence of patient attachment style on self-care and outcomes in diabetes.' *Psychosomatic Medicine 66*, 5, 720–728.

Cree, M. (2010) 'Compassion focused therapy with perinatal and mother-infant distress.' *International Journal of Cognitive Therapy 3, Special Section: Compassion Focused Therapy*, 159–171.

Dinkler, L., Lundström, S., Gajwani, R., Lichtenstein, P., Gillberg, C. and Minnis, H. (2017) 'Maltreatment-associated neurodevelopmental disorders: A co-twin control analysis.' *The Journal of Child Psychology and Psychiatry 58*, 691–701.

Feeney, J.A. (2000) 'Implications of attachment style for patterns of health and illness.' *Child: Care, Health and Development 26*, 4, 277–288.

Felitti, V.J., Anda, R.F., Nordenberg, D., Williamson, D.F., *et al.* (1998) 'Relationship of childhood abuse and household dysfunction to many of the leading causes of death in adults. The Adverse Childhood Experiences (ACE) Study.' *American Journal of Preventive Medicine 14*, 4, 245–258.

Gunnar, R. M. and Vazquez, M. D. (2001) 'Low cortisol and a flattening of expected daytime rhythm: Potential indices of risk in human development.' *Development and Psychopathology 13*, 515–538.

Halligan, S.L., Murray, L., Martin, C. and Cooper, P.J. (2007) 'Maternal depression and psychiatric outcomes in adolescent offspring: A 13-year longitudinal study.' *Journal of Affective Disorders 97*, 145–154.

Independent Care Review (2022) Accessed on 28/9/2023 at https://www.gov.uk/government/publications/independent-review-of-childrens-social-care-final-report.

Mäntymaa, M., Puura, K., Luoma, I., Salmelin, R., *et al.* (2003) 'Infant–mother interaction as a predictor of child's chronic health problems.' *Child: Care, Health and Development 29*, 3, 181–191.

Meins, E., Fernyhough, C., Russell, J. and Clark-Carter, D. (1998) 'Security of attachment as a predictor of symbolic and mentalising abilities: A longitudinal study.' *Social Development 7*, 1, 1–24.

Mueller, S., Maheu, F., Dozier, M., Peloso, E., *et al.* (2010) 'Early-life stress is associated with impairment in cognitive control in adolescence: An fMRI study.' *Neuropsychologia 48*, 3037–3044.

Neff, K. and McGehee, P. (2010) 'Self-compassion and psychological resilience among adolescents and young adults.' *Self and Identity 9*, 3, 225–240.

Raque-Bogdan, T.L., Ericson, S.K., Jackson, J., Martin, H.M. and Bryan, N.A. (2011) 'Attachment and mental and physical health: Self-compassion and mattering as mediators.' *Journal of Counselling Psychology 58*, 2, 272–278.

Sainsbury Centre for Mental Health (2009) *The Chance of a Lifetime: Preventing Early Conduct Problems and Reducing Crime*. Accessed on 13/6/23 at www.centreformentalhealth.org.uk/publications/chance-lifetime and www.wsipp.wa.gov/ReportFile/881/Wsipp_Benefits-and-Costs-of-Prevention-and-Early-Intervention-Programs-for-Youth_Summary-Report.pdf.

Selwyn, J., Wijedasa, D. and Meakings, S. (2014) *Beyond the Adoption Order: Challenges, Intervention and Adoption Disruption*. Department for Education research report. Accessed on 19/1/23 at www.gov.uk/government/publications/beyond-the-adoption-order-challenges-intervention-disruption.

Tacon, A. (2003) 'Attachment experiences in women with breast cancer.' *Family and Community Health 26*, 2, 147–156.

Tacon, A., Caldera, Y. and Bell, N. (2001) 'Attachment style, emotional control, and breast cancer.' *Families, Systems and Health 19*, 3, 319–326.

Tarren-Sweeney, M. (2010) 'Concordance of mental health impairment and service utilisation among children in care.' *Clinical Child Psychology and Psychiatry 15*, 481–495.

van IJzendoorn, M.H. and Juffer, F. (2005) 'Adoption is a successful natural intervention enhancing adopted children's IQ and school performance.' *Current Directions in Psychological Science 14*, 6, 326–330.

Glossary

Abuse Acts that cause harm to another person, whether this be emotional, sexual or physical

ADHD Attention deficit hyperactivity disorder, a diagnosis given where children are overactive and/or impulsive and/or unable to concentrate

Adoption A permanent placement with a new family where one or more adults take on the legal rights of being the child's parent

Adrenaline A chemical messenger preparing the body for activity

Ambivalent A pattern of insecure attachment where the child becomes clingy and is not able to show age-appropriate autonomy because they do not feel reassured enough

Amygdala An almond-shaped nodule in the inner section of the brain concerned with more primitive functions such as sensing threat

Arousal How ready your body is for fight or flight

Attachment The relationship you have with your main caregiver, and the template this gives you for how relationships work

ASC Autism spectrum conditions, a range of presentations of neurodiversity of varying severity, typically involving difficulties with social skills, communication and the flexibility of thinking

ASD Autistic spectrum disorder, now known as ASC

Asperger syndrome An ASC in which the person does not have learning disability or any language delay and the difficulties may be less marked than classical autism

Attachment disorder A diagnostic label given if a child struggles to form a healthy relationship with new carers because of past abuse and/or neglect and falls into one of two specific patterns in how they relate to others

Attunement Being able to hold someone else in mind, pick up their signals in a sensitive way and care about their experience

Avoidant A pattern of insecure attachment where the child avoids relying on anyone else or showing any feelings; they may act as if they are tough and self-sufficient

Black out Lose consciousness

Boundaries Consistent and clear rules

CAMHS Child and Adolescent Mental Health Service, a UK acronym for a team of professionals in each local area who work with children's mental health issues as part of the NHS

Care Living in public care, in a foster family or residential home, rather than your family of origin

Caregiver A parent, adoptive parent, foster carer or person who takes on the primary care of a child

CAT Cognitive Analytic Therapy, a model of therapy developed by Dr Anthony Ryle to address dysfunctional relationship patterns and personality disorders

CBT Cognitive Behaviour Therapy, a very well-evidenced model of therapy where you work on changing thoughts, feelings and behaviours, often using small experiments to test your assumptions

Chaotic Unpredictable to the point of feeling unsafe

Chronic Developmental Trauma A diagnostic category related to post-traumatic stress disorder proposed by Bessel van der Kolk for children who were exposed to chaotic and harmful care for a prolonged period of time

Claiming narrative A story in which you tell the child about the care they deserved and how you would have provided this

Clinical psychologist A regulated mental health professional, typically trained to doctorate level, with expertise in mental health and development (including neurodiversity). They can undertake detailed assessments, develop formulations to help explain what is going on and design and deliver therapeutic interventions

Co-regulate Help the child to set their level of arousal to an appropriate level by matching the caregiver's

Coercive control A form of domestic violence in which an individual asserts control over another person or makes them dependent and fearful through threats, humiliation or intimidation **Consequences** Positive and negative things that we do in response to what the child does when trying to shape their behaviour

Cortisol A chemical messenger in the brain and nervous system related to sensing threat

DBT Dialectical Behaviour Therapy, a model of therapy developed by Marsha Linehan to address chronic patterns of dysfunction including self-harm and inability to tolerate distress

DDP Dyadic Developmental Psychotherapy, a parent-child therapy developed by Dan Hughes to help enhance the attachment relationship and allow the child to develop along on a more positive trajectory

Developmental level Where the child is up to in their development (note that this may not match their chronological age)

Disorganised A category of insecure attachment where the caregiver has been chaotic and/or harmful and no single (organised) strategy of relationship pattern has worked to meet the child's needs

Domestic violence Verbal, physical or sexual violence against a family member or someone living or staying within the same household

Dopamine A chemical messenger in the brain associated with action and rewards

Dyspraxia Difficulty in getting the brain to coordinate and sequence body movements, which typically shows as clumsiness and needing active concentration to complete any motor activity

Dysregulation A state in which a person's emotions are out of their control and their body is in a state of increased arousal

Earned secure A category of adult attachment where the person has been able to reflect on their poor early care experiences and learn a healthier template for relating to other people. Research shows that parents within this category do almost as well with their children as those whose childhoods put them in the secure category

Empathy The ability to understand how other people feel

Expressed need What is communicated directly

Fight, flight, freeze The ways a child learns to behave when there is a threat: they can either attempt to fight it off physically, run away from it or become still and watchful until the threat has passed

Formulation A word for a map of the contributing factors that influence someone's presentation, normally including the predisposing risk factors, the maintenance cycles and the symptoms and behaviours that are produced as a result

Foster carer Someone who cares for a child (normally one who is not blood related or previously known to them) but has not been legally awarded the full rights of a parent, which usually means a social worker will need to be involved in making all major decisions about the child

Good enough parent A legal phrase used to describe a parent who is adequate and does not cause their child to be harmed due to their care

High functioning autism An old-fashioned term for an ASC in which the person is of above-average intelligence, which gives them a better chance of successful independent living in adulthood than classical autism

Hyperarousal Being constantly in a state of increased readiness for fight or flight

Hyperkinetic disorder In the previous edition of the European International Classification of Diseases (ICD) this was the equivalent to the American (DSM) diagnostic category of ADHD, although the criteria were said to be more stringent. In the new ICD, the criteria are more aligned

Innate Something you are born with

Insecure A less healthy relationship with a caregiver who is not consistently available and attuned

Intuitive Done by instinct

Kinship A placement with someone known to the child, such as a member of their extended family (e.g., an uncle, aunt or grandparent) or their wider network (e.g., a neighbour, teacher or family friend)

Learned secure See 'earned secure'

Learning difficulty A specific area of difficulty in learning, such as dyslexia

Learning disability Having an IQ below 70, which is in the bottom 2 per cent of the population and is considered to be a disability

Looked after In public care

Maltreatment Being treated badly

Narrative Story

Neglect Not doing the things necessary to ensure the safe and healthy development of a child (e.g., keeping the environment clean, providing regular food, meeting medical needs, accessing education and providing appropriate social experiences)

Neurodevelopmental A word used to describe conditions that are to do with the way the brain develops

Neurodivergence A term used to refer to any difference from the typical brain. This may include having autism, ADHD or other neurodevelopmental conditions

Nurture Attuned loving care that meets the emotional and psychological needs of the child

Organised Used to describe an insecure attachment pattern that is applied consistently and does not reach the threshold of being unusual or harmful enough to cause concern

Oxytocin A chemical messenger associated with love, sex, skin contact and feeling safe and soothed

Paradoxical Doing the opposite of what is expected

Plastic Able to change

Prefrontal cortex The area of the brain above your eyes, associated with self-monitoring, planning, sequencing, understanding cause and effect, empathy and other sophisticated thought patterns underlying social skills

Psychiatrist A medical doctor specialising in mental health

Psychologist Someone who is highly trained in mental health and therapy but not medically qualified

Quasi-autistic A term for children who appear autistic due to severe and chronic neglect

Reassurance A message that you are okay, and help to regulate and feel confident to go out and explore once again

Reflection Actively thinking about things in a different way

Reflective capacity The degree to which we are able to think about our experiences, thoughts, feelings, behaviours and patterns of relating to others

Regulate Return the level of arousal to a resting state

Resilience The ability to cope with stress and challenges

Schema A belief about the fundamental nature of yourself, the world and other people

Secure A healthy relationship with an attuned and predictable caregiver

Secure base A person who is able to provide attunement and reassurance and help you to regulate

Self-image The way we understand ourselves and how good we feel about who we are

Self-regulate Being in control of your own emotions and able to soothe yourself when distressed so that you do not stay in too high a state of arousal for too long

Sensory integration A process promoted by occupational therapists for helping children to organise sensory information

Shame A belief that you are inherently flawed, bad or unlovable

Strange situation A task used to study the relationship between infants and their parents. It involves the parent leaving the room and returning and looks at the infant's reaction to the separation and reunion

Theory of mind A term used to refer to having a model of how minds work, which allows a person to guess the thoughts and feelings of another person and better understand their behaviour

Theraplay A therapy technique developed by Ann Jernberg and Phyllis Booth within the Head Start scheme in America, in which the parent and child engage in playful interactions to enhance attachment, self-esteem, trust in others and joy within their relationship

Transgenerational Passing from one generation to the next, grandparent to parent to child

Trauma Significant negative experiences that caused the child to fear for their safety

Trigger Any source of stress or reminder of past experiences that can set off patterns of thoughts, feelings or behaviours

Unconscious Outside of the person's awareness, not deliberate

Underlying need A need that is not communicated directly

References

Ainsworth, M. D. S., Blehar, M. C., Waters, E. and Wall, S. (1978) *Patterns of Attachment: A Psychological Study of the Strange Situation.* Hillsdale, NJ: Earlbaum.

Appleyard, K. and Osofsky, J. D. (2003) 'Parenting after trauma: Supporting parents and caregivers in the treatment of children impacted by violence.' *Infant Mental Health Journal 24,* 2, 111–125.

Archer, C. and Gordon, C. (2006) *New Families, Old Scripts: A Guide to the Language of Trauma and Attachment in Adoptive Families.* London: Jessica Kingsley Publishers.

Banyard, V. L., Rozelle, D. and Englund, D. W. (2001) 'Parenting the traumatized child: Attending to the needs of nonoffending caregivers.' *Psychotherapy: Theory, Research, Practice, Training 38,* 1, 74–87.

Bhreathnach, E. (2006) *Parent-Child Engagement, a Co-Regulation Process.* Keynote address at the third National Conference for Occupational Therapists in Child and Adolescent Mental Health, Northampton.

Bond, S. B. and Bond, M. (2004) 'Attachment styles and violence within couples.' *The Journal of Nervous and Mental Disease 192* 12, 857–863.

Burns, L. H. (1990) 'An exploratory study of perceptions of parenting after infertility.' *Family Systems Medicine 8,* 2, 177–189.

Caltabiano, M. and Thorpe, R. (2007) 'Attachment style of foster carers and care giving role performance.' *Child Care in Practice 13,* 12, 137–148.

Carlson, V., Cicchetti, D., Barnett, D. and Braunwald, K. (1989) 'Disorganized/ disoriented attachment relationships in maltreated infants.' *Developmental Psychology 25,* 4, 525–531.

Carpenter, G. L. and Stacks, A. M. (2009) 'Developmental effects of exposure to intimate partner violence in early childhood: A review of the literature.' *Child and Youth Services Review 31,* 8, 831–839.

Cleaver, H., Unell, I. and Aldgate, J. (1999) *Children's Needs – Parenting Capacity: The Impact of Parental Mental Illness, Problem Alcohol and Drug Use, and Domestic Violence on Children's Development.* London: The Stationery Office.

Cozolino, L. (2002) *The Neuroscience of Psychotherapy: Building and Rebuilding the Human Brain.* New York: W.W. Norton.

Crittenden, P. M. (1997) 'Truth, Error, Omission, Distortion and Deception: The Application of Attachment Theory to the Assessment and Treatment of Psychological Disorder.' In S. M. C. Dollinger and L. F. Dilalla (eds) *Assessment and Intervention Across the Lifespan.* Hillsdale, NJ: Erlbaum.

Davis-Kean, P. E. (2005) 'The influence of parent education and family income on child achievement: The indirect role of parental expectations and the home environment.' *Journal of Family Psychology 19*, 2, 294–304.

Dinkler, L., Lundström, S., Gajwani, R., Lichtenstein, P., Gillberg, C. and Minnis, H. (2017) 'Maltreatment-associated neurodevelopmental disorders: A co-twin control analysis.' *Journal of Child Psychology and Psychiatry 58*, 691–701.

Dodge, K. A., Bates, J. E. and Pettit, G. S. (1990) 'Mechanisms in the cycle of violence.' *Science 250*, 1678–1683.

Dozier, M., Higley, E., Albus, K. and Nutter, A. (2002) 'Intervening with foster infants' caregivers.' *Infant Mental Health Journal 25*, 541–554.

Dozier, M., Lindhiem, O. and Ackerman, J. (2005) 'Attachment and Biobehavioral Catchup.' In L. Berlin, Y. Ziv, L. Amaya-Jackson and M. T. Greenberg (eds) *Enhancing Early Attachments*. New York: Guilford Press.

Felitti, V. J., Anda, R. F., Nordenberg, D., Williamson, D. F., Spitz, A. M. and Edwards, V. (1998) 'Relationship of childhood abuse and household dysfunction to many of the leading causes of death in adults. The Adverse Childhood Experiences (ACE) Study.' *American Journal of Preventive Medicine 14*, 245–258.

Fonagy, P., Steele, H. and Steele, M. (1991) 'Maternal representations of attachment during pregnancy predict the organization of infant-mother attachment at one year of age.' *Child Development 62*, 891–905.

Fonagy, P., Steele, M., Steele, H., Higgitt, A. and Target, M. (1994) 'The Emanuel Miller Memorial Lecture 1992: The theory and practice of resilience.' *Journal of Child Psychology and Psychiatry 35*, 2, 231–257.

Ford, T., Vostanis, P., Meltzer, H. and Goodman, R. (2007) 'Psychiatric disorder among British children looked after by local authorities: Comparison with children living in private households.' *British Journal of Psychiatry 190*, 4, 319–325.

Gass, K., Jenkins, J. and Dunn, J. (2007) 'Are sibling relationships protective? A longitudinal study.' *Journal of Child Psychology and Psychiatry 48*, 2, 167–175.

Glaser, D. (2001) 'Child abuse and neglect and the brain: A review.' *Journal of Child Psychology and Psychiatry and Allied Disciplines 41*, 1, 97–116.

Golding, K. (2008) *Nurturing Attachments: Supporting Children Who Are Fostered and Adopted*. London: Jessica Kingsley Publishers.

Golding, K. and Hughes, D.A. (2012) *Creating Loving Attachments: Parenting with PACE to Nurture Confidence and Security in the Troubled Child*. London: Jessica Kingsley Publishers.

Grandin, T. (2006) *Thinking in Pictures*. London: Bloomsbury Publishing Plc.

Grandin, T. (2008) *The Way I See It: A Personal Look at Autism and Asperger's*. Arlington: Future Horizons Inc.

Grandin, T. and Scariano, M. M. (2005) *Emergence: Labelled Autistic*. New York: Warner Books.

Hart, R. and McMahon, C. A. (2006) 'Mood state and psychological adjustment to pregnancy.' *Archives of Women's Mental Health 9*, 6, 329–337.

Hoghughi, M. and Speight, A. N. P. (1998) 'Good enough parenting for all children: A strategy for a healthier society.' *Archives of Disease in Childhood 78*, 4, 293–296.

Holmes, B. and Silver, M. (2010) 'Managing behaviour with attachment in mind.' *Adoption and Fostering Journal 34*, 1, 65–76.

Howard, L. M., Kumar, R. and Thornicroft, G. (2001) 'Psychosocial characteristics and needs of mothers with psychotic disorders.' *British Journal of Psychiatry 178*, 5, 427–432.

Howe, D. (2005) *Child Abuse and Neglect: Attachment, Development and Intervention.* Basingstoke: Palgrave Macmillan.

Hughes, D. A. (2006a) *Building the Bonds of Attachment: Awakening Love in Deeply Troubled Children* [DVD].

Hughes, D. A. (2006b) *Building the Bonds of Attachment: Awakening Love in Deeply Troubled Children.* New Jersey: Jason Aronson.

Hughes, D. A. (2007) *Attachment-Focussed Family Therapy.* London: W.W. Norton.

Hughes, D. A. (2017) *Building the Bonds of Attachment: Awakening Love in Deeply Traumatized Children: Awakening Love in Deeply Traumatized Children* [third edition]. Maryland: Rowman & Littlefield.

Hughes, D. A., Golding, K. and Hudson, J. (2017) *Healing Relational Trauma with Attachment–Focused Interventions – Dyadic Developmental Psychotherapy with Children and Families.* London: W.W. Norton.

Kaniuk, J., Steele, M. and Hodges, J. (2004) 'Report on a longitudinal research project, exploring the development of attachments between older, hard-to-place children and their adopters over the first two years of placement.' *Adoption & Fostering Journal 28,* 2, 61–67.

Lacher, D., Nichols, T., Nichols, M. and May, J. C. (2012) *Connecting with Kids through Stories: Using Narratives to Facilitate Attachment in Adopted Children* [second edition]. London: Jessica Kingsley Publishers.

Lansford, J. E., Cappa, C., Putnick, D. L., Bornstein, M. H., Deater-Deckard, K. and Bradley, R. H. (2017) 'Change over time in parents' beliefs about and reported use of corporal punishment in eight countries with and without legal bans.' *Child Abuse and Neglect 71,* 44–55.

Lichtenstein Phelps, J., Belsky, J. and Crnic, K. (1998) 'Earned security, daily stress and parenting: A comparison of five alternative models.' *Development and Psychopathology 10,* 1, 21–38.

Matsueda, R. L. (1992) 'Reflected appraisals, parental labelling, and delinquency: Specifying a Symbolic Interactionist Theory.' *American Journal of Sociology 97,* 6, 1577–1611.

McMahon, C. A., Tennant, C., Ungerer, J. and Saunders, D. (1999) 'Don't count your chickens: A comparative study of the experience of pregnancy after IVF conception.' *Journal of Reproductive and Infant Psychology 17,* 4, 345–356.

Mills, K. (1998) *Something Better for my Children: The History and People of Head Start.* Dutton: New York.

Nummenmaa, L., Glerean, E., Viinikainen, M., Jääskeläinen, I. P., Hari, R. and Sams, M. (2012) 'Emotions promote social interaction by synchronizing brain activity across individuals.' *Proceedings of the National Academy of Sciences of the United States of America 109,* 24, 9599–9604.

O'Connor, T. G., Heron, J., Golding, J., Beveridge, M. and Glover, V. (2002) 'Maternal antenatal anxiety and children's behavioural/emotional problems at 4 years: Report from the Avon Longitudinal Study of Parents and Children.' *The British Journal of Psychiatry 180,* 6, 502–508.

Read, J., van Os, J., Morrison, A. P. and Ross, C. A. (2005) 'Childhood trauma, psychosis and schizophrenia: A literature review with theoretical and clinical implications.' *Acta Psychiatrica Scandinavica 112,* 5, 330–350.

Reder, P. and Lucey, C. (2000) *Assessment of Parenting: Psychiatric and Psychological Contributions.* London and New York: Routledge.

Rosenthal, R. and Jacobson, L. (1968) 'Pygmalion in the classroom.' *The Urban Review 3,* 1, 16–20.

Rothman, B. K. (1986) *The Tentative Pregnancy*. New York: Penguin.

Roy, P., Rutter, M. and Pickles, A. (2004) Institutional care: Associations between overactivity and lack of selectivity in social relationships. *Journal of Child Psychology and Psychiatry 45*, 4, 866–873.

Runyan, D. K., Shankar, V., Hassan, F., Hunter, W. M., *et al.* (2010) 'International variations in harsh child discipline.' *Pediatrics 126*, 3, e701–e711.

Rutter, M., Kreppner, J., Croft, C., Murin, M., *et al.* (2007) 'Early adolescent outcomes of institutionally deprived and non-deprived adoptees. III. Quasi-autism.' *Journal of Child Psychology and Psychiatry 48*, 1200–1207.

Sanapo, M. S. and Nakamura, Y. (2011) 'Gender and physical punishment: The Filipino children's experience.' *Child Abuse Review 20*, 39–56.

Sansone, R. A., Furukhi, S. and Wiederman, M. W. (2012) 'History of childhood trauma and disruptive behaviours in the medical setting.' *International Journal of Psychiatry in Clinical Practice 16*, 1, 68–71.

Saunders, R., Jacobvitz, D., Zaccagnino, M., Beverung, L. M. and Hazen, N. (2011) 'Pathways to earned security: The role of alternative support figures.' *Attachment and Human Development 13*, 4, 403–420.

Siegel, D. J. (2006) 'An interpersonal neurobiology approach to psychotherapy: Awareness, mirror neurons, and neural plasticity in the development of well-being.' *Psychiatric Annals 36*, 4, 248–256.

Slade, A. (2005) 'Parental reflective functioning: An introduction.' *Attachment and Human Development 7*, 3, 269–281.

Teicher, M. H., Andersen, S. L., Polcari, A., Anderson, A. M., Navalta, C. P. and Kim, D. M. (2003) 'The neurobiological consequences of early stress and childhood maltreatment.' *Neuroscience & Biobehavioral Reviews 27*, 1–2, 33–44.

Tronick, E. (1986) 'Interactive mismatch and repair: Challenges to the coping infant.' *Zero to Three 6*, 1–6.

U.S. Department of Health and Human Services (HHS) (2022) *Head Start Program Facts: Fiscal Year 2021*. Accessed on 13/6/23 at https://eclkc.ohs.acf.hhs.gov/about-us/article/head-start-program-facts-fiscal-year-2021.

Uylings, H. B. M. (2006) 'Development of the human cortex and the concept of "critical" or "sensitive" periods.' *Language Learning 56*, Suppl., 59–90.

van der Kolk, B. A. (2005) 'Developmental trauma disorder: Towards a rational diagnosis for children with complex trauma histories.' *Psychiatric Annals 35*, 5, 401–408.

van IJzendoorn, M. (1995) 'Adult attachment representations, parental responsiveness, and infant attachment: A meta-analysis on the predictive validity of the Adult Attachment Interview.' *Psychological Bulletin 117*, 3, 387–403.

van IJzendoorn, M. H., Juffer, F. and Duyvesteyn, M. G. C. (1995) 'Breaking the intergenerational cycle of insecure attachment: A review of the effects of attachment-based interventions on maternal sensitivity and infant security.' *Journal of Child Psychology and Psychiatry and Allied Disciplines 36*, 225–248.

van IJzendoorn, M. H., Schuengel, C. and Bakermans Kranenburg, M. J. (1999) 'Disorganized attachment in early childhood: Meta-analysis of precursors, concomitants, and sequelae.' *Development and Psychopathology 11*, 225–249.

Wearden, A., Peters, I., Berry, K., Barrowclough, C. and Liversidge, T. (2008) 'Adult attachment, parenting experiences, and core beliefs about self and others.' *Personality and Individual Differences 44*, 5, 1246–1257.

Webster-Stratton, C. (2006) *The Incredible Years: A Guide for Parents of Children 2–8 Years Old* (revised). Canada: Umbrella Press.

Welsh, B. C. and Farrington, D. P. (2007) 'Save children from a life of crime.' *Criminology & Public Policy 6*, 4, 871–879.

Werner, E. E. and Smith, R. S. (1992) *Overcoming the Odds: High Risk Children from Birth to Childhood*. Ithaca: Cornell University.

Winnicott, D. (1953) 'Transitional objects and transitional phenomena.' *International Journal of Psychoanalysis 34*, 89–97.

Winnicott, D. W. (1965) *The Maturational Process and the Facilitative Environment*. New York: International Universities Press.

Wolfe, D. A., Crooks, C. V., Lee, V., McIntyre-Smith, A. and Jaffe, P. G. (2003) 'The effect of children's exposure to domestic violence: A meta analysis and critique.' *Clinical Child and Family Psychology Review 6*, 3, 171–187.

Zagar, R. J., Busch, K. G. and Hughes, J. R. (2009) 'Empirical risk factors for delinquency and best treatments: Where do we go from here?' *Psychological Reports 104*, 1, 279–308.

Zeanah, C. H., Keyes, A. and Settles, L. (2003) 'Attachment relationship experiences and childhood psychopathology.' *Annals of the New York Academy of Sciences 1008*, 1, 22–30.

Zigler, E. and Muenchow, S. (1994) *Head Start: The Inside Story of America's Most Successful Educational Experiment*. New York: Basic Books.

Additional Reading

Recommended books for non-birth-parent carers wishing to learn more about caring for children who have experienced trauma, abuse and neglect or improving attachment relationships:

Caroline Archer and Christine Gordon – *New Families, Old Scripts: A Guide to the Language of Trauma and Attachment in Adoptive Families* (Jessica Kingsley Publishers)

Adele Faber and Elaine Mazlish – *How to Talk So Kids Will Listen and Listen So Kids Will Talk* (Piccadilly Press Ltd)

Adele Faber and Elaine Mazlish – *How to Talk So Teens Will Listen and Listen So Teens Will Talk* (Piccadilly Press Ltd)

Sue Gerhardt – *Why Love Matters: How Affection Shapes a Baby's Brain* (Routledge)

Kim S. Golding – *Everyday Parenting with Security and Love: Using PACE to Provide Foundations for Attachment* (Jessica Kingsley Publishers)

Kim S. Golding – *Nurturing Attachments: Supporting Children who are Fostered or Adopted* (Jessica Kingsley Publishers)

Kim S. Golding and Daniel A. Hughes – *Creating Loving Attachments: Parenting with PACE to Nurture Confidence and Security in the Troubled Child* (Jessica Kingsley Publishers)

Angela Hobday, Angela Kirby and Kate Ollier – *Creative Therapy for Children in New Families* (Wiley-Blackwell)

Dan A. Hughes – *Building the Bonds of Attachment: Awakening Love in Deeply Troubled Children* (Jason Aronson)

Dan A. Hughes – *Principles of Attachment-Focused Parenting: Effective Strategies to Care for Children* (W. W. Norton & Co)

Dan A. Hughes, Jonathan Baylin and Daniel J. Siegel – *Brain-Based Parenting: The Neuroscience of Caregiving for Health Attachment* (W. W. Norton & Co)

Denise Lacher, Todd Nichols, Melissa Nichols and Joanna C. May – *Connecting with Kids Through Stories: Narratives to Facilitate Attachment in Adopted Children* (Jessica Kingsley Publishers)

Daniel J. Siegel – *The Developing Mind: How Relationships and the Brain Interact to Shape Who We Are* (Guilford Press)

Margot Sunderland – *What Every Parent Needs to Know: The Incredible Effects of Love, Nurture and Play on Your Child's Development* (Dorling Kindersley)

Carolyn Webster-Stratton – *The Incredible Years* (Incredible Years/Umbrella Press)

Carolyn Webster-Stratton and Martin Herbert – *Troubled Families – Problem Children: Working with Parents – A Collaborative Process* (Wiley-Blackwell)

Index